CREST FOUNDATION

THE
MOTHER
EARTH

Only Lifeline We Have
Let Us Bring Her Back To Life

S. POCHENDER

STARDOM BOOKS

www.StardomBooks.com

STARDOM BOOKS
A Division of Stardom Publishing
and infoYOGIS Technologies.
105-501 Silverside Road
Wilmington, DE 19809

FIRST EDITION JUNE 2022

STARDOM BOOKS

A Division of Stardom Alliance
105-501 Silverside Road Wilmington, DE 19809, USA

www.stardombooks.com

Stardom Books, United States
Stardom Books, India

THE MOTHER EARTH

S. Pochender

p. 204
cm. 13.5 X 21.5

Category: HOM022000 House & Home : Sustainable Living

ISBN: 978-1-957456-07-2

Dedicated To My Mother

CONTENTS

ACKNOWLEDGMENTS

I have always nurtured a dream of authoring two books. One which would glean out useful anecdotes from my four decades of professional experience and the other, with purely academic intent on the topic of Climate Change. However, never could I think of penning down a book about our planet while making it useful to my fellow brethren. I show my gratitude to Mr. Rajendra Kumar, fellow Director of CREST FOUNDATION who made this idea into reality. The idea floated, the subject was decided, broad contours were discussed and the timeline was set. I am thankful to Mr. Raam Anand for showering his all-pervasive enthusiasm and trust in me. Additionally, I thank Atrayee and the whole team of Stardom without whom, my author journey would have been a half-baked loaf. Krishna J. has always been like a storehouse of unique pieces of art and ideas and I thank him for the stunning book cover. I shall remain indebted to the CREST team for all the brainstorming discussions we had and which always added something new to my perspective.

PREFACE

We humans have always been proactive in satiating our needs. Whether inside the womb or jostling in the outer world, we leave no stone unturned. It took centuries to condition our minds to develop this animal instinct; we get what we need without paying two hoots to the consequences. However, everything around can sustain only on the principle of giving and taking. In fact, research on the mother-fetus relationship has concluded that while the mother's womb supports the fetus with nourishment, the fetus leaves an imprint by repairing many damaged tissues of the mother. It has always been a symbiotic relationship between the mother and the child. However, is this symbiosis visible between humans and Mother Earth? No. Over the centuries, humans have been exploiting every resource available on Earth only for their benefit. We are no longer satiating our needs but have fallen prey to our greed. We, humans, have snatched so much from Mother Earth that she no longer seems to find her balance to sustain. Being the most intelligent creature on Earth, we must understand that Mother Earth is the only lifeline we have, and right now, our lifeline is hanging by a few strands.

This piece of work reminds us of the critical situation Mother Earth is facing and how we can channel our next course of action to save us and our only lifeline.

INTRODUCTION

Finally!!! You got some time to lounge on your newly bought beanbag and open your laptop. The rug on the floor looked a little old and you immediately clicked on amazon to check for a new rug. That touchpad of your laptop did not seem to work well. You open another tab on Google to check for the latest model available. The big drawing-room in your apartment failed to receive much Sunlight as a multistoried residential complex was coming up on the other side. Oh! So much dust. You immediately closed the balcony door and switched on the lights—the three tube lights and the Murano crystal-embellished chandelier, all at once. Why? Just to admire the beauty of the piece! Aah! Now everything looks picture perfect. You cannot find a better portrayal of peace, comfort, and safety.

Now, let us dig a little deeper.

That imported beanbag is made up of expensive leather, non-biodegradable chemicals, and dyes. While you paid a hefty customs duty, Mother Earth was crushed further by a stout carbon and water footprint. When you switched on extra tube lights and the chandelier unnecessarily only to admire your room, you added an extra burden on the whole cycle of electricity production. Now, when you plan to change your two-year-old laptop, do you think of repairing the existing one? No. Why? Because repairing is not worth it when you can get a new one by adding just Rs 5000 more to the repair cost.

1

With your purchasing power, you are after all contributing to the economy. The new dress you bought for your daughter had been the source of income for that company's employees. You have been paying all your bills on time and have been considerate toward paper wastage by opting for online payments. You never litter the roads; you neither waste any water nor do you throw your waste into the water! You are the epitome of an ideal citizen; then why and how are you to be blamed for causing any damage to the environment? You have worked hard enough to afford all the luxuries of life; then why should you be blamed for something that you do not find yourself doing?

Your consumption rate merely reflects the inherent human nature to seek comfort in life while contributing to human development. But are YOU the only person causing the problem? Definitely not. It is the larger collective issue that is being referred to here. We are a part of a larger society. So, if 10 individuals act like you, you are no longer a mere statistic but part of the larger anomaly. Similarly, if one small organization fails to reduce its excesses along with a hundred other corporations, all of them are to be blamed equally, if not more.

The human mind has been instrumental in fostering change and development over the years in the form of the Industrial Revolution. In our pursuit to grow and prosper, we have forgotten the significance of the symbiosis between nature and human life. We have come a long way from being hunter-gatherers to considering Apple as a smartphone. We have drastically altered Earth's ecosystem and food chain while almost irreparably damaging the thriving conditions for flora and fauna.

With industrialization and the concurrent exorbitant use of fossil fuels, we encroached into an avenue that went out of nature's understanding and control. Humans named it 'The Economy,' and it was never a part of the natural ecosystem; however, it interacted with nature and its resources in the most pernicious of ways. In our chase to prove ourselves as the most intelligent creations of God, we have caused much irrevocable damage to Mother Earth.

In turn, we left only a small fraction of a rapidly vanishing natural ecosystem that is somehow not grossly disrupted by human enterprise. This transformation of humans from being an indisputable part of nature to becoming a perilous parasite is the biggest threat to Mother Earth today. Our planet is undergoing a horrifying change in its natural climate cycle due to the logarithmic rise in anthropogenic activities. This change has been dubbed by scientists as 'Climate Change.' Climate usually changes as a result of geologic activities. We humans, however, have accelerated this process due to our indiscriminate consumption patterns. In retrospect, the growth of the global economy seems homologous to the growth of cancer cells or how a virus reproduces within a host.

We have been on a mission of exploiting nature in every way possible way just to satiate our needs. Today, as humanity faces the wrath of nature in the form of drastic weather changes, unnatural wildfires, droughts, and unseasonal flooding, it is high time we humans pay attention to the writing on the wall. The brutal truth about the climate crisis is that we could have slowed down this juggernaut. Nature has been feeding all of us irrespective of our nationality, creed, or color, and now, it is our turn to pay her back. Nature is everyone's business and none of us can shirk away from our responsibility to heal Mother Earth.

If you still wonder, what can WE commoners do, then let me tell you right now that our house is on fire… And it is never too late to turn the tide.

"One of the first conditions of happiness is that the link between man and nature shall not be broken."
—Leo Tolstoy

Pṛtvīm mā hiṃsiḥī

Do not do violence to the Earth

(Yajurveda (YV XII.18)

PART I
OUR HOUSE IS ON FIRE

1

CLIMATE CHANGE: WHY TO BE CONCERNED?

"Man is suddenly becoming aware that by an ill-considered exploitation of nature, he risks destroying it and becoming in his turn the victim of this degradation. Not only is the material environment becoming a permanent menace - pollution and refuse, new illness and absolute destructive capacity - but the human framework is no longer under man's control, thus creating an environment for tomorrow which may well be intolerable. This is a wide-ranging social problem which concerns the entire human family."
— Pope Paul VI

Humankind is staring at the black void of extinction. We can no longer selfishly exploit the finite resources on Earth. Now, the time is to look beyond treating our Mother Earth as a mere commodity. As Barack Obama once stated, *"Climate change is no longer a problem far-off. Climate change is real, and it is happening here and happening now."* The very symptoms of a deteriorating Earth are visible in every stratum of human life.

Do you feel the haphazard and drastic changes in seasons all around the year? Winters are shortening but growing bitter with each passing year. Every summer seems hotter than the last while the news channels beam into our homes the images of the melting glaciers in the polar icecaps. The groundwater level is dropping at a constant rate as there prevails a sheer dearth of rainwater. Don't we see this dearth widening with each passing year? A reduced state of rainfall has been preventing the constant refilling process.

It was a regular affair for our planet to go through alternating warming and cooling phases. Even before humans first appeared on Earth, there had been a sequential alteration in the Earth's climate. The solar system and Earth's geographical markers have played around several natural instigators to cause the changes in Earth's atmosphere.

The Sun's intensity, volcanic eruptions, and changes in naturally occurring greenhouse gas concentrations are considered the natural causes of climate change. However, since the mid-20th century, climatic changes have grown to a considerable state of seriousness. According to NASA, even though natural causes play a role today, their influence is limited while explaining the rapid warming seen in recent decades.

We have to understand that the Earth's climate system mechanics are simple. The energy from the Sun is reflected off the planet, goes back into space, and helps the Earth remain warm enough to sustain the growth of different species. When the Earth absorbs the Sun's energy beyond a certain level, or when atmospheric gases prevent the heat released by the planet from radiating into space, i.e., the greenhouse effect, the planet warms. Both natural and human activities influence the Earth's climate system. Unfortunately, humankind has now taken the reigns and has been damaging Mother Earth in the most brutal way.

Let us understand that climate change is defined as a significant variation of average weather conditions– becoming warmer or drier over several decades or more. Then why are we listening to the news of record floods, raging storms, and deadly heat?

Believe it or not, climate change has manifested itself in a motley of ways and is experienced by every living being, if not equally. The disastrous appearance of climate that we face today is a global affair. If one corner of the human world is getting submerged under mystifying rainfall, the other corner is witnessing a brutal paucity of potable water. The long-term, irreversible change in the climate differentiates climate change from mere natural weather variability.

Knowing Mother Earth

Our majestic blue marble, the home for humans, has more water than one could surmise, considering the scarcity of drinking water. The Earth appears blue in the solar system due to the prevalence of water on the planet's surface. Water makes up about 71% of the Earth's surface, while the other 29% consists of continents and islands. While 96.5% of all the Earth's water is contained within the oceans as saltwater, the remaining 3.5% is freshwater lakes and frozen water locked up in glaciers and the polar ice caps. 69% of the freshwater again takes the form of ice. Did you know if all that ice melts, the sea levels will rise to an altitude of 2.7 km, if Earth's surface was perfectly smooth?

Aside from the water that exists in ice form, there is also an incredible amount of water beneath the Earth's surface. If you were to gather all the Earth's freshwater together as a single mass, it would measure about 1,386 million cubic kilometers in volume. The origin of water on the Earth's surface and the fact that it has more water than any other rocky planet in the Solar system are two long-standing mysteries concerning our planet. The freshwater bodies are responsible for making the land arable. Earth has 15.749 million square kilometers of arable land, plowed or tilled regularly under a crop rotation system. Considering the different countries, India has the most arable land in the world, followed by the United States, Russia, China, and Brazil. If we look at the growth of the human race, the natural resources of Earth, water, and arable lands have helped several human civilizations grow and prosper.

The human race, which started as a hunter-gatherer species, gradually thrived as a food producer through agriculture. Turn the pages of history and explore the sites of archelogy, and we will be bestowed with the tales and records of how civilizations grew across the banks of rivers. Be it Mesopotamia, the Egyptian civilization, or our Indus Valley civilization, we humans could become the most intelligent and the dominant form of life only by exploiting Earth's resources.

Humans treaded through many lifestyles – hunter, agriculturist, followed by the industrial revolution, which became the foundation and guiding light behind all the present-day luxuries. Earth has been the reservoir for our food and energy. Since the discovery of fire, humans have utilized all kinds of combustible resources to satiate their energy needs. In the form of coal, petroleum, or natural gas, fossil fuels have been thoroughly exploited to bring about and advance the industrial revolution. As the human population grew on the bosom of the Earth, their demands kept growing exponentially without paying two hoots to the impending disaster of deforestation, exhaustion of fossil fuels, excessive pollution, and global warming.

It is invariably assumed and indeed true to some extent that the Earth system is a self-regulatory system. In the book called The Anthropology Of Sustainability: Beyond Development And Progress, the concept of self-regulatory mechanism of the Earth system is well described. Being self-regulatory signifies that despite drastic disruption in the physical, chemical and biological constituents of the Earth system, it can be brought back to its natural state. The various component of the earth system works in constant cohesion within a complex feedback system to restore whatever is damaged. However, this restoring phenomenon would have worked wonders if human interventions were not so caustic and assaultive. We humans encroached and ran riot to land, oceans, coastal regions and disrupted the very ecological balance. Water cycle and other biogeochemical cycles have been altered only to satiate human unending needs.

The Acrid Change In The Climate

As per the self-regulatory mechanism, the natural drivers should have pushed our planet toward a cooling period. However, human activities snatched a bigger role in changing the natural greenhouse gas emission level. Over the last century, the constant burning of fossil fuels like coal and oil has increased the atmospheric carbon dioxide concentration. We have to understand that the simple combustion process that helps us run a motor or turbine also contributes to greenhouse gas emission. It is a process that combines carbon with oxygen in a controlled fashion only to give out carbon dioxide as a waste. Moreover, clearing land for agriculture, industry, and other human activities have also been a major contributor to greenhouse gas concentrations.

The consequences of changing the natural atmospheric greenhouse are difficult to predict; however, some of the effects are clearly visible. When we kept releasing the greenhouse gases like carbon dioxide into the atmosphere, we hampered Earth's capacity to keep the global temperature at check. These gases in turn formed a layer much like an impermeable tent. Now, it allows Sun's heat to touch the Earth's surface but does not allow it to go back, resulting in an enormous amount of trapped heat. With each passing year, this trapped heat keeps raising the global temperature. On average, Earth is becoming warmer, and warmer conditions lead to more evaporation and rainfall. However, the timing and amount of rainfall has become increasingly unpredictable. This change has made some places wetter and some dryer. A stronger greenhouse effect has started warming the ocean and partially melting the glaciers and ice sheets, and in turn, the sea levels are rising. Hence, ocean water shall expand if it warms, contributing further rise to the sea levels.

Although changing climate is a natural phenomenon and is an ongoing phenomenon bound to bring meagre change over a period of hundred years. The present climate change scenario, which we call contemporary climate change, is distinctly rapid and far more dreadful.

The contemporary climate change includes global warming and impacts our Earth's weather patterns. The increase in the emission of greenhouse gases, mostly carbon dioxide and methane, is the leading cause for such a change. Apart from burning fossil fuels for energy generation, agricultural practices, steelmaking, cement production, and forest loss are some of the additional causes of this drastic alteration in the climate. Without digging deep into the technical aspects of global warming, let us understand that the greenhouse gases are transparent to Sunlight, allowing it to heat the Earth's surface. As Earth gets heated up, it causes changes like the loss of Sunlight-reflecting snow cover, and thus, global warming is amplified.

Recent environmental studies reveal that temperatures have risen about twice as fast as the global average of the last two centuries. Deserts are expanding, and heat waves and wildfires are becoming more common. There have been around 58,765 wildfires in 2020 alone. There has been increased warming in the Arctic, leading to the melting of permafrost, glacial retreat, and sea ice loss.

Higher temperatures are responsible for more intense storms and other weather extremities. Now, is it limited to only climate or the weather patterns alterations?

The answer is a resounding NO. Every form of life is dramatically affected due to climate change. Many species have come nearer to extinction in places such as coral reefs, mountains, and the Arctic as their natural habitat condition has changed. There are famous images of polar bears floating on broken shelves of ice. Have you forgotten about that iconic image of a famished polar bear shrunken to its bones?

As humans, we nourish and nurture the mentality of NIMBY – Not In My Backyard, We stare at our television screens enraptured while watching a faraway island get washed off by a terrible flood; however, we do not wish to accept the reality of climate change. Do you know wildfires in Western North America are becoming increasingly worse? Summer wildfires have become 80 days longer than it was a decade ago.

Droughts have become more pronounced now, making it easier for fuels to dry out and fires to ignite and spread. Extreme weather events, marked by dry fuels, lightning storms, and strong winds, are also increasingly common and provide essential ingredients for rapid fire growth. Whether we live in the most powerful nation of the World or the poorest of the countries, we all are facing drastic changes in our lives.

Do we not find an increase in the number of lightning strikes? Lightning occurs more frequently when it is hotter than when it is colder. As the global temperature increases, scientists have predicted that the number of lightning strikes will increase by about 12% for every increased degree of change in the global average air temperatures.

Essentially, the changes we witness in our climate are all a part of a vicious cycle where one change leads to another. It is as if we have ticked on the first domino and have fallen prey to all these consequences. Climate change threatens people with food and water scarcity, increased flooding, extreme heat, more disease, and economic loss. Scientists have blamed climate change on human migration too.

And, considering the impact of climate change, it is imperative to tag it as a global phenomenon accentuated by human activities. Let us pause for a moment and ponder. If your house is on fire, what will you do? Will you try to extinguish the raging flame, or will you pack your bags to another place? Human migration can never be a solution. How far can we go? The problem has been an outcome of our outrageous and blatant actions. If we fail to change our mindset or actions, wherever we go, we will set off another fire. If we humans continue the same kind of mindless activities without considering the aftereffects, no corner in this world can be immune to climate change.

As per NASA's global climate change report, the industrial activities of modern human generation have raised atmospheric carbon dioxide levels from 280 parts per million to about 417 parts per million in the last 151 years.

A panel of NASA scientists concluded that there is a greater than 95 percent probability that human-produced greenhouse gases such as carbon dioxide, methane, and nitrous oxide have caused much of the observed increase in Earth's temperatures over the past 50-plus years. As per the World Health Organization, climate change has become the greatest threat to global health in the 21st century. Even if efforts to minimize future warming are successful, some effects will continue for centuries, like rising sea levels and warmer, more acidic oceans. The body of evidence for climate change is resilient and convincing, and multiple lines of evidence are present to pin the blame on human actions. Certain facts cannot be denied, and we have to find a way to steer the problem to its bottom without escaping from our responsibility. It is high time we all understand that the crisis does not belong to any political party or any specific green brigade. We all are an irrefutable part of this problem and have been a cause at some or the other point in our life.

Why Human Activities Are To Be Blamed

We are bound to assume that changes in the Sun's energy output could cause the climate to change since the Sun is the fundamental source of energy that drives our climate system. In fact, studies show that solar variability has played a role in past climate changes. For example, a decrease in solar activity along with an increase in volcanic activity did help trigger the Little Ice Age between approximately 1650 and 1850, when Greenland cooled from 1410 to the 1720s and glaciers advanced in the Alps. However, several lines of evidence prove that the current global warming is not an outcome of the changes in energy from the Sun. Since 1750, the average amount of energy coming from the Sun has either remained constant or increased very slightly.

If the Sun were the culprit, there would have been warmer temperatures in all layers of the atmosphere. Instead, cooling in the upper atmosphere and a warming at the surface and lower parts of the atmosphere have been observed.

Why? Because, as explained earlier, greenhouse gases are trapping heat in the lower atmosphere. Climate models that include solar irradiance changes cannot be held responsible for this temperature trend over the past century or more without factoring in a rise in greenhouse gases.

We have been taught in schools that the atmosphere of Earth is composed of 78% nitrogen, 21% oxygen, 0.9% argon, and 0.04% carbon dioxide and trace gases. How do these gases come to our atmosphere? The current composition of the atmosphere of the Earth is an outcome of billions of years of biochemical modification of the paleo-atmosphere by living organisms. Most organisms use oxygen for respiration; lightning and bacteria perform nitrogen fixation to produce ammonia that is used to make nucleotides and amino acids; plants, algae, and cyanobacteria use carbon dioxide for photosynthesis. The layered composition of the atmosphere minimizes the harmful effects of Sunlight, ultraviolet radiation, solar wind, and cosmic rays to protect organisms from genetic damage. Certain gases in the atmosphere block heat from escaping.

Long-lived gases that remain semi-permanently in the atmosphere and do not respond physically or chemically to changes in temperature are actually forcing climate change. Let us have a look at the gases which contribute to the greenhouse effect.

Water vapor: It is the most abundant greenhouse gas. Water vapor increases as the Earth's atmosphere warms, but so does the possibility of clouds and precipitation, making these some of the most important feedback mechanisms to the greenhouse effect.

Carbon dioxide: A minor but very important component of the atmosphere, carbon dioxide is released through natural processes such as respiration and volcanic eruptions and through human activities such as deforestation, land-use changes, and burning fossil fuels. Humans have increased atmospheric carbon dioxide concentration by 48% since the Industrial Revolution. This is the most important long-lived force of climate change.

Methane: It is another added culprit to the environment through several human activities. It is produced through natural sources and human activities, including decomposition of waste in landfills, agriculture, especially rice cultivation, and ruminant digestion and manure management associated with domestic livestock. Methane is considered a far more active greenhouse gas than carbon dioxide, and is much less abundant in the atmosphere.

Nitrous oxide: It is a powerful greenhouse gas that is produced by soil cultivation practices, especially during the use of commercial and organic fertilizers, fossil fuel combustion, nitric acid production, and biomass burning.

Chlorofluorocarbons: It is a synthetic compound entirely of industrial origin used in several applications. It is now largely regulated in production and released to the atmosphere by international agreements because it is responsible for ozone depletion.

Higher atmospheric carbon dioxide levels have both positive and negative effects on crop yields. Elevated levels of carbon dioxide can increase plant growth. However, other factors, such as changing temperatures, ozone, and water and nutrient constraints, may more than counteract any potential increase in yield. If the optimal temperature range for some crops are exceeded, earlier possible gains in yield may be reduced or reversed altogether. Climate extremes, such as droughts, floods, and extreme temperatures, lead to crop losses and threaten the livelihoods of agricultural producers and the food security of communities worldwide. Weeds, pests, and fungi can also thrive under warmer temperatures, wetter climates, and increased carbon dioxide levels depending on the crop and ecosystem. Climate change is indeed leading to an increase in weeds and pests. A rise in carbon dioxide levels does reduce the nutritional value of most food crops by reducing the concentrations of protein and essential minerals in most plant species.

Climate change has caused new diseases to emerge, affecting plants, animals, and humans. It poses new and unknown risks for food security, food safety, and human health. Now, who has to be blamed for this? The policymakers who concentrate on building a country's economy or the industrialists who release those toxic gases into the air? The answer is everyone. Even you and I. We all are contributing to this bigger problem.

The Haunting State Of Affairs

Let us have a quick look at the evidence of change. The present state of our Earth is terrible, and the condition is worsening with each passing day. The evidence is unmissable as we can see in the following global warming report.

- Global Temperature Rise: Our Earth's average surface temperature has risen about 1.18°C since the late 19th century. This rise is mainly driven by the increased carbon dioxide emissions into the atmosphere and other human activities. Most of the warming occurred in the past 40 years, with the seven most recent years being the warmest while 2016 and 2020 are tied for the warmest year on record.

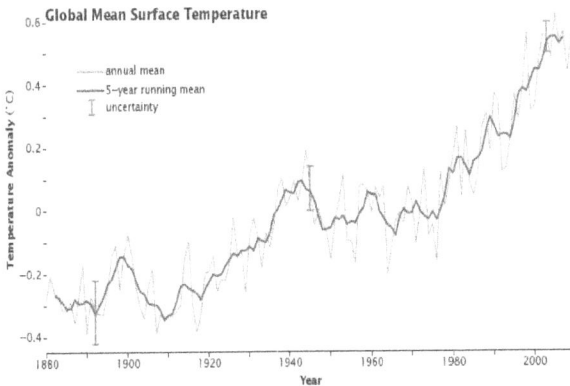

Global Mean Surface Temperature

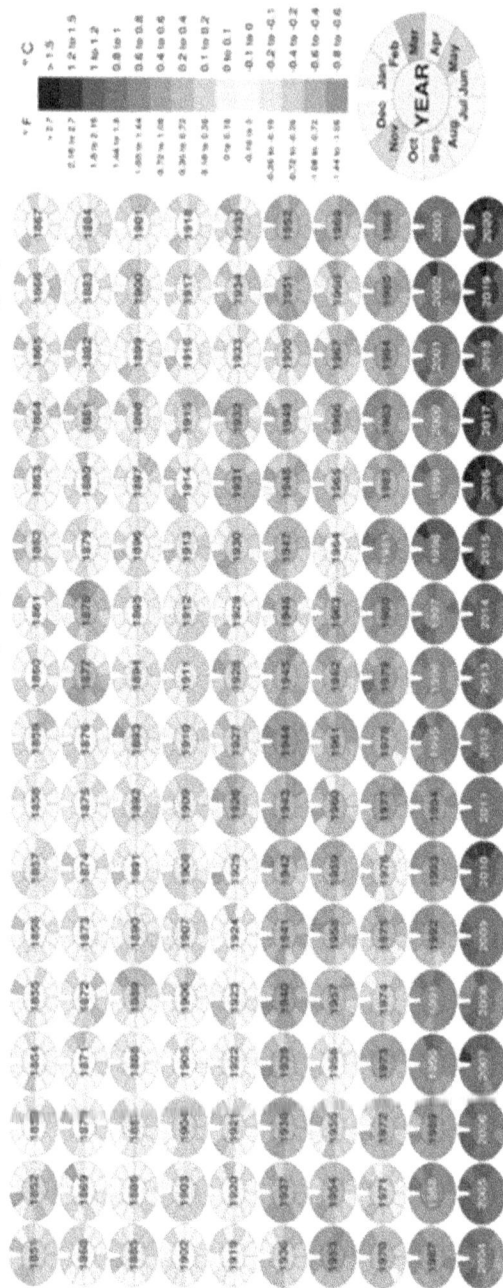

Monthly global mean temperature 1851 to 2020 (compared to 1850-1900 averages)

Data: HadCRUT5 - Created by: @neilrkaye

- Warmer Oceans: The oceans have absorbed much of this increased heat as the top 100 meters of oceans show warming of more than 0.33°C since 1969.

- Shrinking Sheets of Ice: NASA's Gravity Recovery and Climate Experiment proved that Greenland had lost an average of 279 billion tons of ice per year between 1993 and 2019, while Antarctica is losing about 148 billion tons of ice per year.

- Retreating Glaciers: Be it the Alps or Himalayas, the Andes or Appalachian, retreating glaciers and disappearing snowcaps have become a common sight from space. Satellite observations reveal that the amount of spring snow cover in the Northern Hemisphere has decreased over the past five decades. The snow is melting earlier and faster than anticipated.

- Rise in Sea Levels: As stated earlier, everything revolves in a vicious cycle of the ultimate apocalypse. Global sea levels rose by about 8 inches in the last century, and shockingly, the rate in the previous two decades has been nearly double compared to the previous century. Moreover, this rate is increasing, making the archipelago nation of the Maldives and other islands more vulnerable to going under the water.

- Extreme Events: The frequency of tsunamis and cyclones has increased drastically. Wildfires and droughts are becoming regular affairs.

- Acidification of Oceans: The oceans have absorbed 20-30% of total anthropogenic carbon dioxide emissions in recent decades, more likely, 7.2 to 10.8 billion metric tons per year. The acidity of the surface water of the oceans has increased by 30% since the advent of the industrial revolution.

- Devastating effects on nature and wildlife: Recent warming has driven many terrestrial and freshwater species towards higher altitudes. A higher atmospheric carbon dioxide levels and an extended growing season have resulted in global warming. On the same note, heat waves and drought have reduced ecosystem productivity in some regions. There are opposing effects on nature's balance. Plants and animals in the ocean have migrated towards the colder poles faster than species on land. Acidification of oceans has adversely affected corals, kelp, and seabirds, making it harder for organisms such as mussels, barnacles, and corals to produce shells and skeletons. And as we know, heat waves have bleached coral reefs. Climate change has caused harmful algal blooms, which in turn has resulted in eutrophication.

- Disruption in food webs: Marine life has been greatly affected by the alteration of the food chain. Coastal ecosystems are under particular stress while half of the global wetlands have disappeared.

Ecological collapse and destruction of habitats: Industrial production, harvesting of natural resources, and urbanization are human contributions to habitat destruction. Agricultural practices, mining, logging, trawling, and urban sprawl have contributed a lot towards terrestrial habitat destruction, which is responsible for species extinction.

The habitat fragmentation process began a few decades ago; however, we ignored it as we were too occupied with satiating our needs. For example, deforestation in the 20th century has destroyed the Giant Panda's habitat in the Sichuan region of China. Islands like New Zealand, Madagascar, the Philippines, and Japan suffer extreme habitat destruction. Similarly, countries like China, India, Malaysia, Indonesia, Japan, and many regions in West Africa have extremely dense human populations, which hardly gives any scope to the growth and spread of natural habitats. One of the consequences of climate change is floods. How are they be connected? The primary reasons are weather and human factors.

It becomes especially trickier as we do not have enough data to analyze floods of the past. This lack of data makes it hard to compare the trends of yore and the trends of today. However, an IPCC (Intergovernmental Panel on Climate Change) report noted that climate change "has detectably influenced" floods. Climate change has impacted several water-related variables, such as snowmelt and rainfall. So, climate change does not cause floods directly. It just adversely affects the factors behind them. Let us have a closer look at how climate change can impact these factors.

The first factor is that there is heavier precipitation. Warmer atmospheres can hold and thus release greater amounts of water. The resulting scenario is such a heavy rainfall, often termed as Rain Bombs. It is like a month worthof rain happening within a day leading to flood like situations in urban areas. The situation becomes so grim that no drainage system can handle the havoc. Don't we see the news of buildings washing off and an otherwise developed urban settlement ruining to grounds?

It has been noted that the average temperature in the United States of America, in the last century, rose by over an average of 1.8° F. It has coincided with the country also becoming 4% wetter. The IPCC report also notes how extreme storms in the Northeastern parts of the US has generated approximately 27 percent more moisture than they did a century ago. August 2016 saw one historical storm hit the state of Louisiana.

The storm dropped about 7.1 trillion gallons of water in the state. You may have heard of the more famous storms like Hurricane Katrina and Hurricane Isaac. The 2016 storm dumped more water in Louisiana than those two storms. For comparison purposes, Hurricane Katrina dumped 2.3 gallons of water, albeit it dumped more water in different states. However, the 2016 storm does not have a name like the two mentioned here. This unprecedented rainfall was not caused due to a known storm. A study by the National Oceanic and Atmospheric Administration (NOAA) determined that these rains were 40 percent more likely and 10 percent more intense because of climate change.

The IPCC report only produces more grim reading. Heavy precipitation events are projected to increase. It is expected to rise to three times the historical average. One such heavy precipitation event is the extreme weather event known as atmospheric rivers. Essentially, the report surmises that air currents from the tropics would come laden with water from the tropics and dump it on the western coasts of America. The consequence, experts predict, will cause 50% more heavy rain by the end of this century.

It is obvious that heavy rains do not automatically mean floods. However, the risk of occurrence of floods only increases. This is especially true in urban areas where flooding can cause severe damage. Forget America; in the past decade, Chennai has seen how floods can cause damage in urban areas. In fact, a study conducted by the Centre for Climate Change and Disaster Management, Anna University, Chennai, has grim predictions for the coastal city. The study has forecast three models which determine that the 1076-kilometer coast of Tamil Nadu will see extreme spells of rainfall in this coming decade.

These extreme spells of rainfall have been attributed to the warming of the Pacific. So, how prepared is the urban Chennai? Not much. In reality, no city is prepared for Rain Bombs. Chennai may have planned many infrastructure projects to combat these floods. There is the much-vaunted Kosasthalaiyar integrated stormwater drain network.

However, worryingly, these projects have been designed to combat rainfalls which dump 7 cm of rainfall per hour or less. Experts, however, estimate that the city may see rainfall that dumps 20 cm of rainfall per hour more frequently this coming decade.

The IPCC report also predicts more frequent hurricanes in this century. It estimates that there could be an 80% increase in category 4 and 5 hurricanes in the Atlantic basin over the next eight decades. Let us gain some perspective on these hurricanes. Category 4 hurricanes are the second most severe according to the Saffir-Simpson Hurricane Scale. Storms of this intensity can generate sustained winds that can go up to 209 to 251 kilometers per hour.

So, what is a sustained wind? It is the wind speed measured for over a minute at the height of 33 feet. If we were to observe these hurricanes in chronological fashion, it can be illuminating. The period of 1851 to 1900 saw 13 such storms, amounting to an average of 0.26 Category 4 hurricanes a year. The next 50 years saw 29 such hurricanes, an average of 0.58 per year.

Twenty-two such hurricanes were observed from 1951 to 1975, an average of 0.88 per year. The next 25 years witnessed 24 more storms, an average of 0.96 per year. How about the period of 2000 to 2020? These two decades witnessed 32 such hurricanes, an average of 1.4 per year. 2017 saw Hurricane Harvey make landfall in Houston, and it would become the wettest storm in over 70 years in the United States of America. Experts estimated that the storm was more intense and prolonged due to the weakened atmospheric currents, a consequence of a warmer atmosphere. The next year saw Hurricane Florence, the second-wettest storm in nearly 70 years. The IPCC report only predicts rainier storms. It estimates that the hurricanes of the future will be 37 % wetter in the center and about 20% wetter 60 miles away from the center.

Rising sea levels may not seem threatening. Our oceans have risen approximately seven to eight inches higher since 1900. A closer look at this figure will only raise the alarm as three of those inches were added from 1993 onwards. However, high tide flooding can cause severe damage if the water starts at a higher level.

High tide flooding has doubled in the past three decades in the United States, and the IPCC report only expects this to worsen in the coming decades. A new IPCC report also has a grim warning for Asian regions, especially for those in the North Indian regions. The sea levels have increased in these regions have faster than the global average. According to the report, if emissions fall but not to low levels, the sea level in Mumbai could rise by 0.12 meters. In contrast, the sea levels rose by 0.4 meters in 2020. If you wish to have a closer pictorial perusal of the report, I encourage you to use the tool developed by NASA's Sea Level Change Team. It has visualized the projections of the report for every possible scenario.

You can see the loss of coastal regions if we were to continue as usual and the different possible scenarios if we accelerate or reduce emissions. If these words seem unbelievable, you can use the tool through this link – https://sealevel.nasa.gov/ipcc-ar6-sea-level-projection-tool.

As mentioned earlier, extreme weather is the consequence of climate change. Look at the incidences of heat waves, deadly floods, and wildfires. There have been only increasing news reports of such extreme events, and there is no sign of abating. Fossil fuels have been burnt from the industrial age. So, the atmosphere has trapped heat for too long. Global average temperatures have risen by 1.2°C. This change may seem minor and not worthy of the alarm experts suggest. However, it would be best to understand average temperatures in the form of a bell curve. One end of the curve signifies extreme heat, and the other end represents extreme cold. The curve represents the bulk temperatures.

Now let us say there is a shift in the curve. What happens to the curve? It shifts more towards the extremes. In this case, the temperatures shift towards extreme heat. One can see the truth in this statement, as heat waves have only become more frequent and intense. A study conducted by researchers at Princeton University has warned that heat waves of sweltering temperatures are only likely to increase in intensity, frequency, and length. One of the consequences of heat waves is droughts. How? Water evaporates at higher temperatures and quickly.

Ironically, this water contributes to very heavy downpours elsewhere. However, as water is evaporated, the ground becomes dry. As the ground heats up, the air above it also warms. Such heat can also cause groundwater supplies to run out quickly. This shortage becomes an acute crisis due to the demands made by farming and humans. A 2020 study published in the Science Journal talks of how climate change caused by anthropogenic activity has driven a mega-drought in the United States. The study estimated that we could attribute 46% of the severity of the drought to human activity.

How can we overlook another consequence of climate change, the wildfires? In most cases, it has been an outcome of errant human actions like campfires and lit cigarettes. One scintilla is all that is needed; however, the issue can be exacerbated by natural conditions influenced by climate change. As discussed earlier, extreme heat can draw moisture from the land.

The result- the vegetation becomes flammable. They become the fuel for wildfires. It also does not help one iota as the heat waves cause snowpack to melt much earlier. It is as if the forest has laid out a red carpet for the inferno to spread rapidly. The issue becomes even more complicated due to the changed meteorological patterns caused by human activity. It means rain-laden clouds are shifted away from wildfire-prone areas.

On the same note, wildfires can also be sufficiently self-serving. It develops so quickly and with such great intensity that it can produce its own weather patterns. Intense wildfires can form pyrocumulonimbus clouds. These enormous clouds produce lightning strikes.

These strikes ignite even more fire. According to Climate Central, forest fires that can cause damage in areas over 40 square kilometers are seven times more likely to occur in Western America compared to the 1970s. Additionally, the loss of vegetation on the earth surface adds fuel to the fire. Vegetation plays a crucial role in delaying the resulting flood and it also helps in percolation of the rain water into the ground water system. As vegetation has reduced, it has increased the chances of rainfall turning into floods.

Extreme rainfall events that have become the new normal these days are also a side dish of climate change. Cities experiencing severe floods even to a normal rain fall is an outcome of reduced vegetation.The usual, unhampered weather cycle would see water be evaporated into the atmosphere. The gaseous vapor becomes droplets and then falls back onto the ground as rain. However, today the weather cycle has been damaged due to climate change. More water vapor has been absorbed, leading to more droplets. It means that certain regions get heavier rainfall and in a shorter space of time.

The news stories of rain wreaking havoc have become more commonplace. In the past decade, we have seen such damage affecting countries like Germany, the Netherlands, Belgium, and China. We have seen similar stories being reported in India as well.

Peter Gleick, a water specialist from the US National Academy of Sciences, told the BBC, *"When areas of drought grow, like in Siberia and western US, that water falls elsewhere, in a smaller area, worsening flooding, like Germany and Belgium."* The weather has always been variable on this planet. It is why people relied on radios, newspapers, and now the internet to keep abreast of the weather. However, climate change has only made it even more complicated.

In 2017, India witnessed one of the most significant climate change events in modern history. It would come to be known as the Great Smog of Delhi. The pollution in the country's capital city had peaked beyond acceptable levels. However, this smog is an ongoing problem and was not unique to that day in November 2017. In fact, both India and China suffer from this problem. One of the best comparison metrics we have is to look at the air quality before and during the lockdown.

A study found that there was a significant and gradual decline in most cities in the two countries during the lockdown. For instance, before the lockdown, five out of six cities had an AQI (Air Quality Index) of 2.5. To put that number into perspective, it represents that the air was unhealthy for the sensitive group category. The only exception was Chennai. The air in Chennai was found to be under the moderate category.

Six weeks into the lockdown, all cities except for Delhi and Lucknow saw significant improvement in air quality. The air was found to be in the good and moderate category. According to the Council on Energy, Environment and Water (CEEW), India has seen an increase in frequency and intensity of extreme weather events by almost 200% since 2005. A study recently published in the Lancet Journal attributes more than 7 lakh deaths in India annually to the extreme hot and cold conditions.

Abhinash Mohanty, the Program Lead at CEEW, remarked, *"More than 80 percent of the Indian population resides in extremely climate-vulnerable districts, but the next big challenge is restricting the temperature increase and halting the primarily human-induced micro-climate change. India's average temperature has risen by around 0.7°C during 1901-2018. The temperature increase has led to severe loss and damage and lowered work productivity that has ravaged lives and livelihoods."*

The Indian governmental report on climate change also does not provide any good news. It talks of how the frequency and intensity of droughts have increased significantly from 1951 to 2016. The report also warned that heat waves could intensify four-fold by the end of this century.

These heat waves can prove critical as groundwater supplies run short. According to a 2019 report published by the World Resources Institute, India is one of the 17 countries with extremely high-water stress. If heat waves increase both in frequency and intensity, the future seems bleak unless action is taken. As the scientific community witnesses global climate change, they concluded that the effects should remain and reverberate beyond this century. The magnitude of climate change beyond the next few decades depends primarily on the amount of heat-trapping gases emitted globally and how sensitive the Earth's climate is to those emissions. And even if we leave aside the scientific connotation, we cannot escape the fact that human life is walking towards an apocalyptic end. Although we are habituated to synonymizing global warming and climate change, global warming is just one ingredient of climate change. Humans have caused major climate changes to happen already.

Each passing year, we widen our waste generation, pollution levels, deforestation, and urbanization rate. This in turn is worsening our Earth's already terrible state. Do we realize that if we stop emitting greenhouse gases today, the rise in global temperatures will begin to flatten within a few years? Temperatures would certainly remain well-elevated for many centuries; however, they shall reach a plateau. These adverse effects of human activities on Earth's climate to date are irreversible.

But, a small effort on a daily basis to reduce the future probability of temperature rise shall essentially add value to our life on Earth. If we don't take the preventive measures, the global temperatures will rise by 2.5 °C to 4.5 °C by 2100. If we recognize the concept of Heaven and Hell, let us understand that humans have slowly created Hell on Earth. Our desire to lead a luxurious life, dependence on technology, and mindless exploitation of natural resources has built a highway towards Hell. And before it is too late to avoid or limit some of the worst effects of climate change, we must hold hands to delay our doomsday.

> *"The environment is where we all meet; where we all have a mutual interest; it is the one thing all of us share."*
> – Lady Bird Johnson

A Quick Fact Check: Climate Hot Spots

The Guardian published an article over the key parts of the world where climate change has been showcasing its devastating effects, and the scientific community could predict the future.

- Murcia, Spain: If the temperature continues to rise to another 2°C, the Mediterranean basin could become a desert, and the ecosystem could go barren for the next 10,000 years.
- Dhaka, Bangladesh: Erosion and saltwater intrusion on low-lying lands may cause five to 10 million people to migrate from the coastal areas in the next 20 years. The flood frequency has increased from 1 in 20 years to 1 in 5 years. Bangladesh is expected to face more droughts and more flooding during the monsoons.
- Mphampha, Malawi: Droughts are becoming more frequent, rains less regular but heavier when they occur; food supplies are less certain, and the dry spells and floods last longer.

The average annual temperatures across southern Africa may increase by 3°C by the 2060s and 5°C by the 2090s. Human life will be nearly impossible to survive in that temperature. Locals must adapt their farming, restore their forests, improve their water supplies and grow their economies quickly to have any chance of surviving climate change.

- Longyearbyen, Norway: The average temperature for the whole of 2016 in Longyearbyen (650 miles from the North Pole) was near freezing, but it is usually −10°C. Water temperatures on Svalbard have increased 10°C or more over 30 years. Temperatures are changing, and snow is melting earlier and taking longer to freeze up. More precipitation is expected in northern Scandinavia, and low-pressure weather systems take a more northern route. The melting of the Greenland ice sheet and the Arctic glaciers and warming of permafrost temperatures is going to increase coastal erosion

- Manaus, Brazil: Hot spells in humid climates are a real hazard to health. Dry seasons are longer by a week than they were a decade ago. There is a 1°C warming in the Amazon and in areas like Rondônia, where widespread deforestation has occurred. There is an additional 1°C warming due to the replacement of forests with pastures.

- New York, US: Spring begins sooner. Winter snow is less, and there are more intense downpours. By the 2050s, sea levels could rise nearly 76 cm, and storm surges and flooding will be more common in coastal areas. Similarly, the West Nile virus and many other diseases could become prevalent.

- Manila, Philippines: Sea-level rise, increasing temperatures, extreme weather events including tropical storms and heat waves, and changes in precipitation would lead to loss of homes and livelihoods, displacement of communities.

The Changing Food System

"The proper use of science is not to conquer nature but to live in it."
—Barry Commoner

The basic tenet of human survival resides in the old adage of sustenance and procreation for the continuity of the species. Of this, sustenance takes precedence because procreation becomes next to impossible without sustenance. Humans have always been pack of animals. Large groups of similar characters have tended to settle in areas which are deemed favorable for sustenance. Initially, the foraging for food was limited to what the land could provide. As time went by, humans realized that the land could be tilled, and the soil could be replenished with artificial nutrients for growing food faster.

As with any human development, the rise in agriculture also led to indiscriminate cutting down of perennial forests, some of which were bio-diversity hotspots. Here, there are two lines of thoughts that might have contributed to the change in the food system. One, when humans accelerated their development, they also inadvertently caused their own consumption habits to change. Earlier, humans were living off of maybe one or one and a half meals a day. As development progressed, so did our eating habits. One meal became two; two became three, and nowadays, people eat whenever they have a mere whim.

This led to the destruction of a lot of forest lands to make way for agricultural land. Cash crops to be grown were the order of the day. Large carbon sinks in the form of trees were wiped out, releasing a lot of the stored carbon back into the atmosphere. Though the crops planted did offset a part of the carbon released, it was minuscule compared to the whole picture. Moreover, the use of inorganic fertilizers degraded soil quality, and the resultant soil runoff leached into the water bodies causing eutrophication. The subsequent algal blooms further played havoc in the marine eco-systems, thereby altering the food chain.

Indirectly, it also contributed to climate change by removing carbon sinks and altering of marine fauna and flora. The second line of thought is a bit more complex to comprehend. This postulates that as and when humans developed, their consumption patterns did not change in type (only in volume), but the anthropogenic activities caused major damage to the food chains.

Picture this scenario. A civilization finds newer resources to exploit for its economy, but it is located underground. Strip mining is performed to extract these resources, but inadvertently, this causes the destruction of agricultural land and extinction of animals that are an integral part of the food chain. The civilization then realizes that other food sources need to be procured to satiate its burgeoning population and then moves to other lands or seas to obtain this elusive food.

They use their resources as a bargaining chip to perform illegal procuring of food from another area while being backed by their own economic and military clout. This also leads to climate change because whole ecosystems are damaged accidentally, and the food system is thrown haywire.The effects of climate change on food systems have been detected worldwide. They are mostly due to warming and shifts in precipitation patterns. Impacts can now be observed on all continents and ocean regions, especially low-latitude and less developed areas facing the greatest risk. Continued global warming has potentially severe, pervasive, and irreversible impacts on people and ecosystems.

The risks are unevenly distributed but are generally greater for disadvantaged people in developing and developed countries. Climate change affects food security. As mentioned before, it can either be a direct or indirect consequence of our own actions. It has led to the destruction of many indigenous crop types, which are susceptible to heat and temperature differences. Moreover, the rising temperatures provide optimum conditions for phytopathogenic organisms to prey on food crops, e.g., Blight of wheat caused by fungi and Blast of rice caused by bacteria. Future warming could further reduce the global yields of major crops by direct heat damage.

Crop production may be negatively affected in low-latitude countries, while effects at northern latitudes may be positive or negative. Up to an additional 183 million people worldwide, particularly those with lower incomes, are at risk of hunger as a consequence of these impacts. Climate change also impacts fish populations. With a rise in global temperatures, the algae present in our oceans flourish and deprive the seawater of oxygen. This, in turn, causes acidification of water due to increased carbon dioxide absorption and thereby causing loss of other marine flora and fauna. It is an open secret that the North Atlantic fishing grounds are almost starved of food fish species due to a combination of global warming and over-exploitation of these fishing grounds.

Closer to Asia, China has seen a rapid decline of its fishing grounds in the South China Sea, thereby forcing them to rely on sub-standard farmed fish or hunt for newer fishing grounds. This has also led to the flaring up of tensions in the neighborhood due to repeated and frequent encroachment on other sovereign nations' maritime boundaries. The rise in global temperatures also brings with it an associated problem. Not only does the population of algae thrive; however, it also leads to an increase in the levels of toxic dinoflagellates in the seawater. When normal food fishes ingest them, the fish die, and when humans consume these dead fishes, it leads to endotoxin poisoning in mankind. Globally, the rise in temperatures will cause a reduction in the number of fish species that can be sourced.

Do You Not See The Change?

"The challenge of pollution and global warming is no longer the science, or the rate of innovation, but the rate of implementation. We have the clean solutions; now let's bundle them and install them."
– Jens Martin Skibsted

A few decades earlier, we used to get rains for a period of one week to two weeks continuously but with a low intensity.

And such events used to occur at least four to five times in one rainy season. It was the source of our groundwater recharging. Do we see such low-intensity long-term rains these days? No. Rains have become sporadic and fail to recharge the groundwater. We have now come to a stage where we need bore wells going up to 1500 feet to fetch water. If the situation worsens further, how much farther humans can dig? Instead of having heavy rainfall occurring for a few hours evenly for at least two to three seasons, we have entire rainfall occurring in just one spell in a season. This is throwing entire cities to flooding risk and throwing all the systems out of gear. Homes getting washed away in cities is the new normal now. Underground car parking is becoming just dangerous without having preventive measures in place.

Municipal authorities are challenged to make the necessary amendments to fit in the changing climatic conditions. Our habits have changed with the advent of technology. Earlier, natural air was replaced by the fan, and now we cannot survive without an air-conditioner. Why? Because humanity is running through the vicious cycle of you-reap-what-you-sow. Our industrious nature to imbibe with technology and comfort, and our selfish exploitation of natural resources have indeed brought in a drastic change in the surrounding environment. Lack of trees, ever-growing pollution, a never-ending queue of waste accumulation have led to this dramatic change in the climate, and we are nearing doomsday. Change is inevitable, but the change must not be fatal to our mere existence.

Whether we like it or not, we cannot escape from acknowledging the drastic change in the climate. While glaring at the hotspots, we are thrust by the fact that the climate is changing faster than anticipated.

The rapidity of climate change is terrifying, and it needs to be arrested; lest humans should be extinct sooner than ever thought of.

2

HUMANS ARE THE NEW PARASITE

"The ultimate test of man's conscience may be his willingness to sacrifice something today for future generations whose words of thanks will not be heard."
— Gaylord Nelson

We humans, thrive for excellence and earnestly work on the principle of making things easy. We fear the convoluted route and try out new things to achieve comfort in the easiest way possible. Considering the exponential diversification in human activities on Earth, we can easily call Home sapiens as the evolving parasite. They are growing and eating away our Mother Earth. Presently, as the world is crying over the Covid pandemic, do you know how an infection occurs to our body? Every disease that is caused by a pathogen carries a more or less similar philosophy. The germ or the parasite thrives inside our body, while sucking out all the resources. The food we eat, the energy we derive are snatched from us, and the parasite feeds on them.

And in this process, as the germ grows inside our human body, we tend to lose our strength. Bereft of our resources, we fall prey to the parasite, which slowly takes away all our abilities to cope. Why am I talking about parasites here? If you dig a little deeper into the grave situation of the present world, you will find an uncanny resemblance between present-day humans and parasites.

The methodological classification considers a parasite as any organism that exists in or on another organism that is called as its host, and benefits from the nutrients obtained at the expense of the other. A possible consequence is that the parasites may exhaust all the resources generating and nutrients, and the host might end up being decayed or dead. Well, it is rather thought-provoking if the concept of the parasite is directly related or contrasted with mankind and earth. Mankind exists on the resources available on earth, and the resources are being exploited to such an extent that the host or the Earth is impacted gravely.

With the evolution of mankind, man has developed various ways of existing within the nature to survive. Man has always been an integral part of the ecosystem. However, in due course of time, he started transforming from being a part of the ecosystem to a disruptive force within the ecosystem. Earth is the home of millions of species, but it is dominated and exploited by only one: The Homo sapiens. Our initiative, ingenuity, and activity have altered practically every aspect of our globe. We are, in fact, having a significant influence on it. Indeed, our intellect, invention, and actions are now the driving forces behind every global issue we confront. And each of these issues is becoming more acute as the world's population approaches ten billion people.

Fact Check! Humans Are Anthropocentric

What do I mean? The prevailing idea is that humans are the most important and central species on the planet, and that other species, plants and animals, were created to fulfill their needs. Humans and all other living things that maintain human life are the emphases of an anthropocentric approach, which ignores a number of other things that do not appear to have any direct worth to people.

Anthropocentrism has a harmful impact on the environment and on sustainable development. The United Nations defined anthropocentrism as development that satisfies the requirements of the current generation without jeopardizing future generations' ability to satisfy their own needs. Humans are relieved of the obligation of caring for the environment or nature when the attention is only on their current generation.

This viewpoint favors advances that suit the demands of today's people regardless of the environmental consequences, and it cares less about the ability of future generations to meet their developmental needs. The way we have been extracting the minerals and fossil fuels unabated and unchecked for years all to satiate our ever-increasing needs, we are hitting the roof with nary a thought to its depletion and concern for the future. We are indiscriminately, extracting and exploiting fossil fuel resources like, coal, oil, gas, and shale, oil sands, etc., to fulfill the present generation's insatiable energy requirements without regard for the impact our actions will have on future generations. We are running out of fuels and also degrading the environment as a result of the dirty techniques we use to produce these resources are examples of such consequences. For decades, anthropocentrism has been the dominant worldview, negatively impacting the environment and causing natural imbalance, climate change, global warming, and environmental degradation.

"Nature doesn't see things through the prism of good or bad. It rewards efficiency. That is the simplicity of evolution, matching design to environment."
–Blake Crouch

Humans cause a variety of effects on the physical environment, including overcrowding, pollution, fossil fuel combustion, and deforestation. Climate change, soil erosion, poor air quality, and undrinkable water have all been further induced by changes like these. These negative consequences can have an influence on human behaviors, resulting in mass migrations or wars for clean water.

When every scientific community has jostled to point out human actions, we are certainly doing something wrong. It can never be propaganda running riot from nowhere. There is certainly some fire to cause this smoke of thoughts.

Why do you think every other corporate house is talking about sustainability? Why is that hullabaloo on a big podium of Climate Summit? We have obviously been doing something wrong in our day-to-day activities that a big bastion of people is raising a voice. From causing pollution to deforestation, we have been the real culprit over the ecological damage.

Humans Have Hastened The Doomsday

In our pursuit of making life easier, we humans have undoubtedly crossed four generations of the industrial revolution. Yes, it is four, and we are currently thriving in the era of improvising the existing technologies to improve our life. The journey of the industrial revolution began with six essential ingredients–high levels of agricultural productivity to feed the booming population, a pool of managerial and entrepreneurial skills, available ports, rivers, canals, and roads to cheaply move raw materials and finished goods.

Not to forget that political stability and a business-friendly legal system also facilitated in building the lifestyle we have right now. Honestly, if Earth is our home, its natural resources are our birth right. However, in the last 50-60 years, humans have probably exploited that birth right while affecting the homeostasis of life on Earth. Let us have a quick look at the natural resources Earth has provided us and how quickly we depleted them.

Fossil fuels: Fossil fuels are formed by the burial of photosynthetic organisms such as plants on land which largely create coal, and plankton in the waters over millions of years which primarily form oil and natural gas. These creatures took carbon dioxide from the atmosphere and the ocean in order to thrive, and their burial stopped that carbon from moving through the carbon cycle.

The burning of this ancient material releases carbon dioxide into the atmosphere at a pace hundreds to thousands of times quicker than it took to bury it and considerably faster than the carbon cycle can remove it. As a result, carbon dioxide emitted by the combustion of fossil fuels accumulates in the atmosphere, with part of it dissolving in the ocean and causing global warming. The great bulk of the world's energy demands is met by fossil fuels.

Oil, natural gas, and coal are examples of fossil fuels that are burned to create energy. This energy is used to produce electricity, as well as to power transportation, such as vehicles and planes, and industrial activities. Our use of fossil fuels has continuously risen since the arrival of the first coal-fired steam engines in the 1700s. Every year, we currently consume approximately 4,000 times the quantity of fossil fuels that were burned in the 70s over the world. The impacts of fossil fuel combustion, particularly carbon dioxide emissions, are having far-reaching consequences for our climate and ecosystems. There are several issues with fossil fuels. By releasing carbon and other greenhouse gases emissions into the atmosphere, burning fossil fuels quickly heats the globe and acidifies the oceans. Air pollution is also caused by the burning of fossil fuels, which kills an estimated 6.5 million people each year. Oil extraction may pollute rivers and create earthquakes; coal extraction can ruin forests and other landscapes, and natural gas extraction can pollute waterways and cause earthquakes.

Water: Is there anything more critical than water to support life? Freshwater may be found on the surface of the Earth in the form of lakes, rivers, and glaciers, as well as below the surface in the form of groundwater. Despite the fact that our globe is 70% water, just a small portion of it is freshwater.

It is a finite resource; it accounts for just around 3% of all water on the planet. Even though freshwater is considered a renewable resource, its consumption in some areas surpasses the natural processes' ability to restore supplies. When the demand for freshwater cannot be satisfied, political tensions and public health issues might arise. It is to meet the basic needs for of our existence.

Apart from utilizing for basic requirements for survival, mankind has indulged in exploiting the water resources extensively for new needs like industrial uses, energy production, etc. Water depletion indicates a lack of water, which signifies that water sources are going dry. Water shortage occurs when freshwater supplies are insufficient to fulfill demand.

It has an impact on every continent. Nevertheless, it is true that the source of freshwater is available in the nature and is accessible in the form of the Hydrological Cycle. The earth's hydrological cycle is the sum of all mechanisms that transfer water from the land and ocean surface to the atmosphere and back in the form of precipitation. The hydrological cycle is influenced by various variables, including seas and land surfaces. The presence of plants enhances the ability of the ground surface to retain moisture. Plants intercept precipitation, which is subsequently instantly evaporated when collected by the canopy.

Through evapotranspiration mechanisms, the plants themselves produce a significant amount of water vapor. The water falls onto the earth's surface as rain and then goes on to fill the natural as well as manmade reservoirs. These, in turn, feed into the groundwater reservoir, with the remaining water runs away into rivers. The rivers transport the water to the sea in the due course. The same water evaporates during summer and during other periods leading to the formation of clouds, and the same water comes back to our earth as rainfall.

This water cycle continues forever. We should know that the entire water budget going through this cycle is fixed. Now we are using this resource as explained earlier in an unplanned manner and in increasingly in larger quantities, thus interfering with the hydrological cycle. The production of food is a necessity for humankind that requires an ample supply of water. For effective and long-term farming, adequate water sources are needed for effective and long-term farming. Crops perish without water, farmers lose revenue, and people go hungry. Irrigated and rain-fed cropping systems are the two types of cropping systems.

Agriculture uses over 70% of freshwater withdrawals. Irrigation, pesticide and fertilizer application, and animal maintenance are just a few of the applications in this area. Water is used for food preservation and processing further down the value chain. While using water cans boosts yields significantly, it also has severe environmental consequences.

Unsustainable resource usage can result in decreased water flows, changes in downstream water availability, increased soil salinity, or the loss of wetlands, which serve essential ecological services such as biodiversity, nutrient retention, and flood control. Furthermore, climate change is already having an impact on irrigated agriculture since water demand is rising while supply is decreasing where irrigation is most required.

Agriculture that relies on rainfall accounts for around 80% of the land under cultivation and generates about 60% of world food. Water scarcity, droughts, and crop failure occur in many places of the world as a result of either too much or too little rain falling at the wrong time. Rain-fed agriculture is a low-input method of agriculture. Productivity can range from moderate to poor depending on total annual rainfall and its distribution and the kinds of soils. Agriculture that relies on rain is more dangerous, as crop failures in dry locations are more likely owing to inconsistent and unexpected precipitation. Rain-fed agriculture is more successful on soils that can store a large amount of water, i.e. loamy and clayey soils.

Did our exploitation of water stop with agricultural purposes? No. We innovated to harvest water to generate electricity by developing Hydropower, often known as hydroelectric power. It is a renewable energy source that creates electricity by altering the natural flow of a river or other body of water using a dam. To generate electricity, hydropower uses the unending, continually replenishing mechanism of the water cycle, which uses a fuel—water—that is neither diminished nor removed in the process. Hydropower plants come in a variety of shapes and sizes, but they are always driven by the kinetic energy of flowing water as it travels downstream. Hydropower converts kinetic energy into electricity using turbines and generators, which is then supplied into the electrical grid to power homes, companies, and industries. To produce electricity, tremendous amounts of water are required. The water is mainly used as a coolant in producing the electricity. The heated water is again cooled in giant coolers and returned to the system to be used for cooling purposes again.

As populations grow and droughts become a worry, the quantity of water used by energy-producing systems becomes increasingly important. Changes in water supplies may also have an influence on the dependability of energy generation. Nevertheless, water quality and flow can be affected by hydropower. Low dissolved oxygen levels in the water caused by hydropower plants are hazardous to riparian or riverbank ecosystems and may be remedied utilizing different aeration techniques that oxygenate the water.

"Water water everywhere, not a drop to drink."
– Samuel Taylor Coleridge.

How Dare I Call Humans A Parasite?

Let us turn a few pages of human history. The year of 1795 will have the first scribbled word on the pages of industrial revolution when humans unleashed the potential of mechanization. The world of agriculture so got revolutionized by industrial belts. The process continued with the second wave of the industrial revolution when humans made electricity, gas, and oil as their sources of energy.

This revolution resulted in the creation of the internal combustion engine that started to reach its full potential. Development of steel demand, chemical synthesis, and methods of communication such as the telegraph and the telephone, the inventions of the automobile and the plane at the beginning of the 20th century made this second wave of the industrial revolution the biggest success of human evolution.

With the third wave, humans introduced nuclear energy, computerization, automation, and robots and precisely, humans loudly proclaimed to be the most intelligent and affluent product of God's creation who could make their lives better. However, do you think other living beings do not make their lives better during their stay on Earth? Of course, they do. They all adapt to new living strategies and evolve in due course of time. Still, the case of humans is quite different as the pursuit to gain, gain and gain comfort seems never-ending and leaves Nature in bad shape. While humans continuously exploit the natural resources and cause a dreadful impact on climate and different ecosystems, should we not call ourselves the parasite leeching on Earth?

A Lifestyle Of Exploitation

With the advent of technologies, human beings have developed the lifestyles benefitting their standard of living that vehemently oppose nature. Humans have lost sight of the fact that they are a vital component of the environment. The ecosystem includes all living and non-living species both visible and unseen, on the planet. To fulfill escalating human demands for resources, like as food, energy, and lumber, the planet is increasingly managed in a way that maximizes the flow of material from nature.

As a result, people have transformed at least 70% of the Earth's terrain, mostly to cultivate plants and maintain animals. These activities require deforestation, land degradation, biodiversity loss, and pollution and have the greatest impact on terrestrial and freshwater ecosystems. Despite supporting millions of people, almost 77 percent of rivers longer than 1,000 kilometers no longer flow freely from source to sea.

Increase in landfills have inhibited many channels and tributaries abruptly. Overfishing is the primary source of ocean change, although other processes such as agricultural runoff and plastic pollution have also had an impact on 66 percent of the ocean's surface.

In the last 150 years, the amount of live coral on reefs has virtually halved, and it is expected to vanish entirely. Coral reef ecosystems are among the most diversified in the world and have been drastically impacted. A country like Columbia is facing a rabid growth of hippopotamus as the drug lord, Pablo Escobar, moved them. As people transfer organisms throughout the planet, the number of alien species, discovered beyond their normal range - has increased, disrupting and frequently diminishing local biodiversity. Many endemic species are also threatened by this and habitat changes caused by humans.

Changes in land and sea usage, exploitation, climate change, pollution, and the introduction of alien species are the primary causes of ecosystem loss. The dumping of rubbish into the ocean, for example, has a direct influence on wildlife. Other factors are more indirect. These include demographic, economic, political, and institutional systems, all of which are based on social ideals and interactions.

For example, enormous swaths of land controlled by Indigenous peoples are seeing ecological loss at a slower rate than the rest of the world. However, Indigenous peoples' rights are under assault, which might hasten the destruction of these ecosystems. This would have a negative influence on ecosystems and societies in general. Since the beginning of the post-industrial age, international trade has intensified, as has the exploitation of living elements from nature. People are oblivious to the harm produced by their consumption due to the increased physical distance between supply and demand.

People had to care for the environment around them before the Industrial Revolution since that's where their products came from. They would suffer the repercussions if man did not take care of it. We now have significant environmental consequences far from where we reside as a result of globalization. However, we are oblivious to these effects because we are protected from them. Inequality is also created and increased through international trade. Human overpopulation has had a long-term impact on the ecosystem and has been a source of concern for scientists.

If the human population continues to grow at its current rate, the planet's food supply will almost likely run out. Much of the damage we have done to the environment has been caused by our inability to accommodate the population boom. Health and abundance have become a new double-edged sword as a result of technological advancements. Our food supply can now feed more people than ever before, and medical innovation has led to longer life spans. However, this fact has the unintended consequence of lowering population turnover and resulting in faster population growth.

As our standard of living and life expectancy grows, so do the issues posed by overpopulation. The need to feed an ever-increasing human population has aided significant advancements in agriculture, which was the first major human innovation to ensure our species' existence. Hunter-gatherer civilizations were able to occupy a region and plant their own food thanks to early agriculture. This had an immediate influence on the ecology since non-native species were transplanted to new places, and particular plants and animals were prioritized for cultivation over others. Recent breakthroughs in genetic modification have sparked worries about newly produced crops' environmental effects.

Domestication of cattle and other creatures, such as dogs and cattles and horses, by early humans, had a huge impact on the ecosystem by modifying the soil. By diminishing native grasses and contributing to soil erosion, grazing animals led to environmental change. And we now know that the fast development of cow populations to fulfill human nutritional demands has significantly influenced the composition of gases in the atmosphere. Agriculture's industrialization over the last several centuries has worsened these consequences, but it has also spawned a surge of counter-movements that attempt to reverse the harmful effects of human interference. People are becoming more aware of the environmental impact of large industrial farms and are seeking to return to smaller farms and even urban gardens. As eating local becomes more fashionable, the urban space is being reclaimed for traditional agriculture.

It is indeed an attempt to go healthier; however, the problem lies in space constraint. Growing populations need the construction of more homes and cities, which necessitates additional land. Forests are frequently cleared to create ways for urban and suburban development, and produce building materials. Every year, it is estimated that 18 million acres of forest are clear-cut to make way for the development and the production of wood products. Basically, we are running through a never-ending malicious cycle of production and consumption.

The Global Forest Review as released during 2021, reflects upon an atrocious loss of forests. The tropics lost 11.1 million hectares of tree cover, including 3.75 million hectares of loss that occurred within tropical primary rainforests. These areas were of critical importance for carbon storage and biodiversity and were equivalent to a rate of 10 football pitches a minute. And it's not just tropical forests that are of concern. Boreal forests — mainly those in Russia — experienced unparalleled tree cover loss in 2021, largely due to wildfires.

Deforestation has several consequences, including reduced oxygen levels and increased greenhouse gas emissions, increased soil erosion risk, and the elimination of animal habitats. However, similar to industrial agriculture, some organizations have attempted to generate a beneficial counter-impact to deforestation's negative environmental repercussions. Reforestation operations aim to replace as much forest area as possible each year, and it is anticipated that less than half of the trees that are cut down each year are replaced.

Human activities impact the environment by contributing to air pollution, whether through vehicles or through industries. Poisonous gases are sent back to the environment without giving two hoots to the consequences. While it can be difficult to determine which pollutants are linked to specific environmental or public health consequences, it is widely acknowledged that air pollution can impair human health as well as plant and animal life. Pollution isn't only confined to the air we breathe.

It comes from human waste, industrial chemicals, and other sources and impacts soil or rivers. These pollutants have a huge impact on the natural world, causing environmental deterioration and issues like acid rain and toxic algal blooms in the ocean.

The production and consumption of fossil fuels, as well as the carbon dioxide emissions that result is one of the most significant ways that people have impacted the environment. Carbon dioxide emissions, according to recent studies, contribute to the deterioration of the earth's ozone layer, which may contribute to global climate change. This is especially true when emissions are combined with the loss of forest lands' carbon-sink effect due to deforestation and existing particulate matter in the air. Though the size and consequences of such climate change are debatable, the scientific community has agreed that human activity has an impact on the global climate to some degree.

Where Lies The Root?

According to the book called The Anthropology of Sustainability: Beyond Development and Progress as edited by Marc Brightman and Jerome Lewis, the present human world relishes an empowering ideology called Neoliberalism. We all, irrespective to our average wallet size are encouraged to lead a life traded over unbridled capitalism.

The early 1970s had witnessed an economic crisis in the US, which in turn had sown the seed of liberalism on a pan-continental basis, thus leading to exploitation of resources only to satiate the overwhelming growth of human race. In our pursuit to excel in life, natural resources have become subservient to this growth. Our needs have metamorphosed into a new avatar altogether and super materialism has strengthened its roots. However, it cannot be one person adding up in his list of needs. The whole process is invariably fueled by population growth and in turn has inflicted a pincer attack upon the Earth's system.

We live in the luxury of technology in the current time, and none of us wishes to stay behind. In our long-cherished pursuit to grab everything around, we have come to a stage where we have more commodities than we need. When the scientific community or the sociologists talk about sustainability, they do not urge us to go bereft of technology. They point out the problem which stems from our very attitude to giving everything a shot. Let's take the example of the ever-growing models of mobile phones. You buy a Samsung Galaxy model, and your mobile phone works perfectly, fulfilling all its roles. Soon, the consumer market dances on the ad of a VIVO model, which apparently has all the features your phone has with a little extra pixel in the front camera. And then?

You vehemently abandon your existing good phone and buy the trending model in the market. What happens to the old phone? It ends up in the scrap and contributes to the overall solid waste disposal. You may ask, how much burden can an extra phone add? Correct, but what if everyone starts thinking the same way? In the end, the effect of disposing of one phone is compounded unbelievably. Let us have a look at our attitude, which has gradually become a threat to our own existence.

Wastage of Food: Over the years, we have started consuming all the resources on a per capita basis while most of the things are ending up as waste For example, if our food consumption is increasing on a global level, does it reflect an increase in health conditions? No. Because the consumption is not evenly distributed globally. While the affluent is busy gathering every kind of food and end up wasting half of it, the poor is hardly able to get one meal a day.

Do you believe that at least 1 5 million tons of cooked food per annum is wasted? It is best not to forget that the wasted food used the same amount of resources as the consumed food in the same quantity. Whether one eats the food or wastes it, it leaves the same amount of carbon and water footprint.

An Over-do with Electricity: Every second household in our community has an AC in all their bedrooms, a microwave, induction stove, washing machine, and almost every other electrical appliance. We shudder in fear if the electricity is cut off for half an hour. Why? Because we have become completely dependent on it. Moreover, have you found our new tendency? We wish to keep the AC at 18°C and cuddle up inside a cozy blanket. Why? It is not about only CFC release in the environment but how we lead our lives. The present way of exploitive mindset reflects on a peculiar temperament. We all are aware of the crisis and still wish to live in that cocoon of comfort.

The Culprit Called Transportation: An affluent family in India has more than two cars, and each member prefers to use their own. Why do you think Delhi had to implement that odd-even rule of vehicles on the road? A car can hold a minimum of four people, and still, everyone wants to travel separately. Let us have a look at this case scenario. A bus can carry 50 people and consumes fuel only twice the cost of a car. Now, when only one man travels in a car, theoretically, he is using up natural resources of up to 25 people. Over the last few decades, public transport has become a mode of travel for those who fail to afford a car. Ridiculous! In a country like Singapore and Japan, even the CEOs of a multinational company would use the trains to commute, then why cannot we? Similarly, air transportation was initially restricted to emergencies and business travels or transport of commodities with low shelf-life. Leaving aside the socialistic viewpoint, people use air transport for simple journeys. Just ask yourself once if the travel is really essential?

The Fickle Nature of Single Use: We humans have been attracted towards the use and throw policy over the years without realizing how much solid waste we are accumulating. While in most of the cases, we consider using biodegradable products, we often forget the burden on the production cycle. Moreover, why do we have to throw things after a single use? Our forefathers lived on the principle of reuse and recycling, so why cannot we?

Instead of using the single-use plastic tumblers, we can obviously reach out to our traditional way of steel or metal tumblers. But we do not do so for we have to wash the metal vessels. This growing tendency of single use is an outcome of our laziness. Another example is repeated buying of bottled water. These days, people carry an uncanny fear towards the water from a water cooler or any stored water, and they end up buying bottled mineral water. In our pursuit to be safer and healthier we end up going for blind purchases that invariably add up to plastic waste.

Filling up the Wardrobe: Whether cotton, wool, polyester, or a blend of it, we are not keeping any cloth for more than six months. Why? Because the fashion trend is changing every now and then. Every corner of the town has a huge shopping mall to attract customers with the latest trendy clothes. Somehow, while running behind the rat race, we have forgotten the pleasure of preserving a grandfather's blazer or an aunt's saree.

The human world is, of course, divided into two distinct sections where one has everything in excess, and the other is hardly able to satiate its basic needs. The privileged must understand the repercussions of a wider production cycle of different products. Our lust to avail everything, whether food or technology, or clothes, invariably increases the production cycle and leaves a lasting impact on carbon and water footprint.

"The consumption society has made us feel that happiness lies in having things, and has failed to teach us the happiness of not having things."
– Elise M. Boulding

What Is Your Carbon Footprint?

The amount of carbon dioxide emissions associated with all the activities of a person or major activities like industries, transportation, etc., constitutes a carbon footprint. Carbon footprint can be caused by direct emissions from fossil-fuel combustion.

The source stems in manufacturing, heating, and transportation and also from every single industrial process. In short, every production cycle of any human activity in today's world leaves behind a carbon footprint. Let me state a hypothetical scenario to drive home this point. You are a prospering farmer in a small village. With all the profits earned over the years, you wanted to refurbish your humble two-bedroom lodgings into a more spacious four-bedroom one.

In the pursuit of achieving this dream, you had to chop down a few trees to expand the built-up area of the house. For the increased number of rooms, more amenities had to be procured. The industries producing these amenities had to increase their production cycles. For the construction, more cement had to be procured, and which also led to the cement factories increasing their production capacity. You are happy that your new house is taking the desired shape, but little do you realize that your actions are increasing your carbon footprint and the carbon footprint of a number of other organizations. It sounds harsh to blame you alone for this but imagine a scenario where a thousand individuals like you perform these actions at the same time. This ballooning effect is what exactly causes a significant increase in the carbon footprint of an area.

Transportation, housing, and food account for most of an individual's carbon footprint. In short, population growth and explosive economic growth especially in industrial sectors have played a considerable role in the Earth's capability to absorb carbon emissions both at land and at sea. Thus, it has become like an indelible footprint that humans are leaving on the surface of the Earth. According to the studies conducted by Centre For Sustainable Systems, University of Michigan which, different human activities leave their carbon footprint in a variety of ways.

The negative impact of anthropocentric activities on the environment is far too much to fit into a few words and describe them concisely. Carbon footprint essentially serves as the indicator of human-induced climate change.

"Like music and art, love of nature is a common language that can transcend political or social boundaries."
—Jimmy Carter

It is produced via air pollution and toxic acid rain. Concomitantly, coastal and ocean acidification is also a byproduct of human actions at a personal and societal level, leading to increased carbon footprint and, consequently, climate change.

In the aforementioned question, 'YOUR' is a generic pronoun that talks about the carbon footprint left at both individual and social levels. Carbon footprint assessment is done on three levels. Level 1 focuses on the direct greenhouse gas emissions resulting from the fuel combustion during production, transportation, process emissions, and fugitive emissions via leakage during production processes.

Level 2 is concerned with the indirect carbon footprint as a result of the consumption of purchased electricity, heat, steaming, and cooling. Finally, Level 3 is associated with greenhouse gas emissions as a result of other indirect activities. These may include purchased raw and finished goods, commuting (personal and business-related), logistics, and waste disposal, trading of goods and allied services, and finally, the financing of these Level 1 and Level 2 operations. For an individual, Level 2 emissions hold more significance.

The calculation includes the emissions associated with goods that are imported into a country but are produced elsewhere and generally take into account emissions associated with international transport and shipping, which is not accounted for in standard national inventories. As a result, a country's carbon footprint includes several indirect components even though it tries to reduce the carbon footprint within its boundaries. It must be reduced at an individual as well as at the social levels. According to the recent studies conducted by Centre For Sustainable Systems at University of Michigan, every ingredient of our consumption leaves a carbon footprint. The following piecharts summarizes the problem:

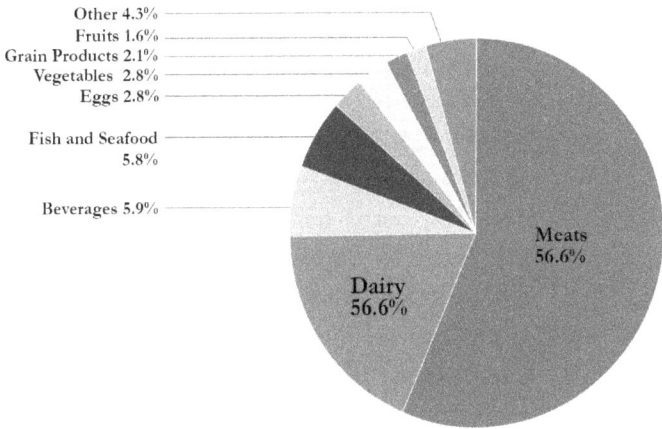

Other 4.3%
Fruits 1.6%
Grain Products 2.1%
Vegetables 2.8%
Eggs 2.8%
Fish and Seafood 5.8%
Beverages 5.9%
Meats 56.6%
Dairy 56.6%

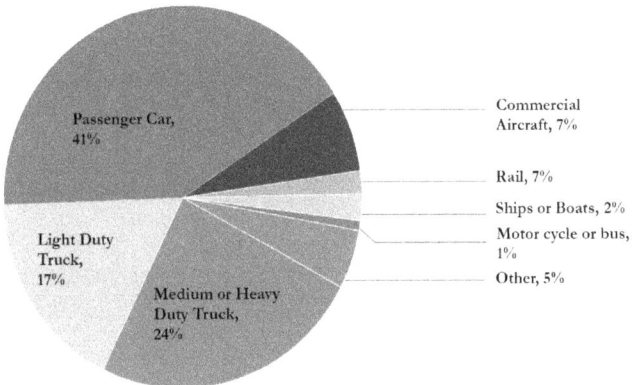

Passenger Car, 41%
Commercial Aircraft, 7%
Rail, 7%
Ships or Boats, 2%
Motor cycle or bus, 1%
Other, 5%
Light Duty Truck, 17%
Medium or Heavy Duty Truck, 24%

One can opt for different strategies to reduce the carbon footprint and contribute to global climate mitigation. Several industries opt for carbon offsets where they invest into carbon-reducing activity or technology.

Carbon footprints can be reduced through improving energy efficiency and changing lifestyles and purchasing habits.

- Switching one's energy and transportation use can impact primary carbon footprints. Take a walk to the next lane instead of getting into your AC car.
- Install energy-efficient lighting insulation in buildings or use renewable energy sources to generate electricity. Have you heard of motion-sensitive lighting? Many universities in Europe, Singapore, and the US have installed that to avoid electricity wastage in the corridors.
- Reduce consumption of meat. The production cycle is overwhelming if looked through the lens of carbon footprint.
- Purchase products that require fewer carbon emissions to produce and transport.
- Service the automobile on a regular basis to keep it running efficiently. Correctly inflated tires can help minimize emissions.
- Use cruise control for long distances and this will help you conserve petrol.
- Carpooling allows you to divide your individual emissions among the number of persons in your vehicle.
- Be vocal for local. Exotic fruits like avocados, kiwi, etc., might taste good, but they are imported, which puts the burden on the carbon footprint due to air/water transportation.

Measuring carbon footprint in terms of the land area does not mean that carbon sequestration is the only way to solve the carbon problem. It simply demonstrates how much bio-capacity is required to handle our untreated carbon waste and prevent a carbon build-up in the atmosphere. This method of measurement allows us to handle the climate change problem holistically, rather than merely shifting the load from one natural system to another.

In truth, the climate crisis arises because the world's bio-capacity has become insufficient to neutralize all carbon dioxide produced by fossil fuels while also meeting the other demands. As environmentalists raise their voice on planting more trees, let's analyze if Earth was not prepared for such a carbon calamity. Forests are Earth's respite to combat human-induced carbon emissions. Rapid deforestation is equivalent to cutting out the lungs of our Mother Earth. Planting trees is an encouraging practice; however, it takes centuries to bring life to a forest, which is a flourishing ecosystem in itself. Planting a few trees today may not come to our rescue in the prevailing crisis.

Before anyone judges my words as preachy, let me share a personal anecdote where I could find the prevailing mindset of humans to ape the trend. Recently, I had paid a visit to my village. A friend of mine had constructed his new house. Although the house was beautiful, I was taken aback by his column slab concrete building.

Bereft of clay tiles with brick walls, the house was far from the village style. A storied house had too much in its construction in this case. Our usual brick-style housing could handle more floors, and my friend could have had thicker walls for insulation. Moreover, the cost would have been half had he constructed brick walls and clay tiles with semi arched roofs. Summers would have been cooler, and winters would have had enough warmth inside the house. When I asked him why, he cited his inclination towards city-styled houses. The concrete structures are hardly breathable, so he needed AC and fans.

Coming to think of it, do you know that our conservative style of housing was apt for our climate? It is healthier and pocket-friendly too. The column bean style is suitable for multistoried buildings, and not for individual housing. This is a typical case of saddling your wallet to follow the trend while overlooking the extraneous damages. I don't have any answer to someone's decision to go for the city-like house; however, with my knowledge and experience, I can see the sheer need to change.

Similarly, the preconceived notion about bottled water is enormous and impermeable. A large sect of people think that bottled water is safer than piped water. This is far from the truth. Piped water in any city or town is freshly supplied everyday or every alternate day and mark my words as an environmentalist, they are absolutely safe.

Alternatively, bottled water, at any given point in time is 15 to 20 days old, considering the timeline from production to shelf. Secondly, despite using PET bottles, plastic does get leached into the water and gets into the human system causing irreparable long term damage to the health of the consumer. A recent study conducted by the Dutch government has concluded that blood samples from almost 70 percent of the population contained plastic remnants. The statistic is for a fairly cold region, so you can imagine the grim situation of a country like India. Bottled waters correspond to extra plastic waste and an added burden to on Earth. Now, whom should we blame for this? How did this fear over piped water crop up?

Every step human take is an outcome of a preconceived notion. Whether we wish to keep our AC on throughout the day or wish to pile up our plastic waste, everything is a reflection of our exploitative lifestyle. Our over-consumption and unthoughtful actions have become a threat, so much so that we are leaving a carbon footprint at both personal and social levels to an extent that is difficult to curtail. A change is the need of the hour.

Change the mindset. Change the way of living. Change the myopic analysis and look at the global crisis

3

IT'S A CRISIS TIME!!!

"When the last tree is cut, the last fish is caught, and the last river is polluted; when to breathe the air is sickening, you will realize, too late, the wealth is not in bank accounts and that you can't eat money."
–Alanis Obomswaim

Could you sense the impending, horrifying state of affairs when you read the previous pages? The present world is screeching out over eco-anxiety. Are you aware of this term? Eco-anxiety is the sense of fear and anxiety about environmental and natural disasters, such as climate change, air pollution, and an imbalanced ecosystem. Cutting one tree inside a boundless forest is a story of humans' dependence on nature; however, running havoc through deforestation is an entirely different tale—a horrifying story to be precise. If we consider our inclination to science and technology as the culprit behind the irrefutable climate change, the same science also tells us that it is not too late to stem the tide. It took several decades to come to this worsening climate condition, and it is never an outcome of one particular human being.

The climate crisis is global, and so is the battle to combat it. As humanity faces down this crisis, personal endeavors shall evolve to social implementations. Climate change is one of the biggest challenges, and it demands some fundamental transformations in all aspects of society. It is high time to reconsider the way we grow food, conserve or waste it. The time has come to restyle our way of living while chalking out an escape route from consumerism, planning for a circular economy to conserve energy, and reducing waste generation. The core idea is to retrospect before adding another digit to the carbon or water footprint data. Technology did contribute to climate change; however, the same technology has helped build new and efficient systems to reduce net emissions and create a cleaner world.

The outlook is gradually moving towards renewable energy while electric cars are poised to become mainstream. An effort to decarbonize the economy will impart us a breathing room as it allows us to mitigate a portion of our carbon footprint while also maintaining the balance in the ecosystem, biodiversity, access to fresh water, improved livelihoods, healthy diets, and food security. Improved agricultural practices, land restoration, conservation, and the greening of food supply chains are some of the essential steps towards combating the crisis. Scalable strategies are the new hope to leapfrog to a cleaner and more resilient world.

If governments, businesses, civil society, youth, and academia work together, we can create a healthier and more sustainable future. As George Bernard Shaw rightly said– Progress is impossible without change, and those who cannot change their minds cannot change anything. At a personal level, we may not be able to bring in drastic progress; nevertheless, we can make some baby steps to build a better future.

The Dire Need Of Sustainability

A few decades ago, sustainable living sounded more philosophical than an urgent need.

Making a positive change and reducing the personal and societal environmental impact to tackle the climate crisis has become a sheer need for the human race. So, is sustainable living a mere method of reducing one's carbon footprint? Yes. If you don't drive a car or do not do much to cause air pollution, are you not contributing anything to the global carbon footprint? You shall be shocked to see your environmental footprint. That extra plate of food that you may have wasted, those extra hours you kept your AC on; you have contributed enough, even though unintentionally. The idea of Sustainable Living is to encourage people to minimize their use of Earth's resources and reduce the damage of human and environmental interactions. Sustainable living is a meshwork of various aspects to maintain a homeostasis between human society, economics, and the environment.

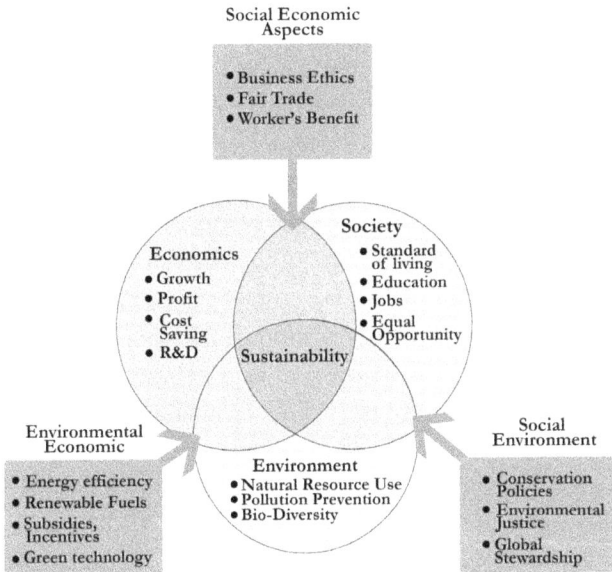

Human existence is indeed dependent on natural resources. We cannot survive without utilizing natural resources.

However, the concept of sustainability helps us to avoid any exploitation while maintaining harmony with the biodiversity. Humans are often hardwired to take refuge in the most comfortable state of living. With proper education and awareness towards climate change, humans must realize the significance of the conservation policies on the global platform. The economic aspects work on the growth and harbor the profit-making attitude. Sustainability is not against economic growth; rather, it works to make an energy-efficient system while implementing the novel idea of circular economy. Economic sustainability is about bringing a balance between economic growth and combating climate crisis. Sustainable living is about preserving the environmental equilibrium, which is often known as net-zero living or making a zero-energy balance with the Earth. The idea is to return to the earth whatever we take from it. But is it possible to achieve a zero environmental impact? Perhaps no.

Moreover, one of the crucial aspects to consider is the influence of societal and economic means while we try to achieve environmental sustainability. Without acknowledging the societal and economic impact, the environmental sustainability plan will collapse. The visionary thinker and economist Kate Raworth has proposed a wonderful concept of Doughnut Economics which encompasses a bigger picture on how our global and local systems can operate within our means as humanity to indulge in sustainable living. In her book, Doughnut Economics, she has proposed various ways to implement sustainable thinking within economic growth. The doughnut of social and planetary boundaries is a serious approach with a touch of humor to frame the challenges in one compass and to strategize wisely.

In words of Kate Raworth, *"Humanity's 21st century challenge is to meet the needs of all within the means of the planet. In other words, to ensure that no one falls short on life's essentials while ensuring that collectively we do not overshoot our pressure on Earth's life-supporting systems, on which we fundamentally depend – such as a stable climate, fertile soils, and a protective ozone layer."*

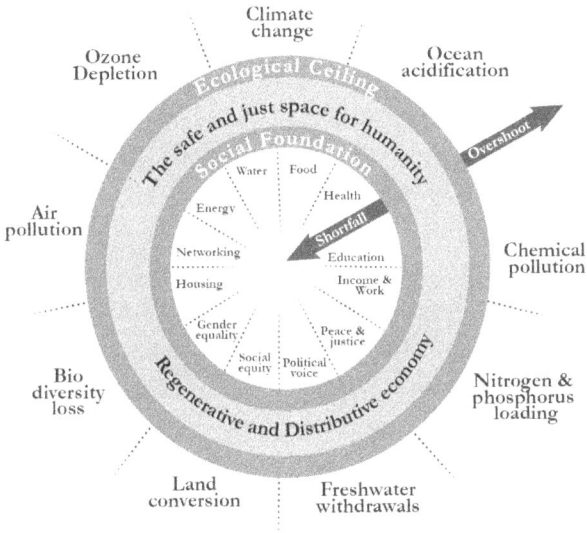

Is There A Protocol For Sustainable Living?

No. There is no perfect blueprint to work with; however, sustainability holds well with many personal interpretations. Many different strategies, actions, and lifestyle tweaks can come together to draw a picture-perfect sustainable way of living; however, none of us can be perfectly sustainable, and the spectrum is wide enough to cover. Some of the common ways to implement a sustainable lifestyle at a personal and societal level can be summarized as follows:

- Opt for renewable sources of energy. The benefits of renewable energy, both environmentally and economically, make it one of the biggest sustainable living solutions.
- Encourage organic farming.

- One of the biggest causes of biodiversity loss is the usage of chemical fertilizers and pesticides.

- Have you lent your thoughts to regenerative agriculture? As consumers, we can choose to purchase from farmers who use organic and regenerative methods. The more of us who are privileged enough to afford the extra cost adopt it, the more these methods will become viable and more affordable.

- Do consider plant-rich diets. Plant-rich diets reduce emissions and tend to be healthier, leading to lower rates of chronic disease. The meat and dairy industry takes up 83% of all farmland and is responsible for 60% of the agricultural industry's 13.7 billion tons of yearly greenhouse gas emissions.

- Reduce food waste by better planning, preserving, and freezing food; find creative ways of using food scraps, composting, and growing your own food. Additionally, buying products close to expiry dates from the supermarket helps prevent them from going straight to landfills.

- Replace gas-guzzling, high horsepower vehicles with fuel-efficient, hybrid, or electric cars.

- Going green while reducing energy consumption helps in saving money. Consider making off-grid homes that utilize renewable energy and naturally collected rainwater, composting toilets, and wood-burning heat.

Aren't We Over-Consuming?

While we note climate change and global warming, there runs a parallel problem of humans' unquenchable thirst for more stuff. Over the 20th century, the world embraced a new ornament of consumerism. The capitalistic mindset transformed every common human into a consumer.

Over the century, humans nurtured this habit of buying every possible luxury as per the trends set by the businesses. The notion of human beings as consumers first took shape before World War I, when the industrial revolution lent out a lot of advanced products to ease the human workload. Common humans gradually realized the need for materials to make their life more convenient and comfortable. The profit-oriented capitalists harvested the increased consumption by the commoners. The traditional objective of making products for their self-evident usefulness was eventually displaced by the goal of profit and became a machine designed to allure consumers.

Considering the percentage perspective of resource consumption, tomorrow will never look any better if today isn't alarming for you. If you go through the OECD review, the global use of materials is increasing fast and might double to nearly 167 Gigatons in 2060. Non-metallic minerals like sand, gravel, and limestone are expected to grow the most, followed by biomass. Overconsumption is not restricted at your personal level but at every step of manufacturing a product for you. Let us take an example of China's construction industry. China has less than 2% of its constructions done with recycled materials. If this linear approach is kept intact, China's housing and road constructions will demand 562 billion tons (twice more than today's) of materials. And that will, of course, bring in more GHG emissions that will be released.

The massive shopping centers in our present world are built upon the premise of endless consumption of products. With endless marketing and advertising, humans are spoon-fed towards their needs. Earlier, a need was the mother of the invention, while now the proverb has taken a new avatar. New inventions come into the market daily and build the need amongst us. In the simplest terms, consumerism is defined as an economic and social ideology and order that encourages consumption or acquisition of goods and services in a never-ending cycle. So, does consumerism encourage purchasing and consuming goods and services over a person's basic needs?

The answer is yes, and consumerism comes with its own set of pros and cons. On the one hand, consumerism drives economic growth and boosts innovation. On the other hand, it instigates problems ranging from environmental and moral degradation to higher debt levels and mental health problems.

The present world is thriving in a consumerist society and let me warn you that humanity is wandering on the stage of an ultra-consumeristic attitude. Humans' love for comfort has unleashed the problem of over-accumulation, which has impacted the environment badly. Simply put– The more you have, the more you leave behind. All that accumulated over the years eventually end up as waste and nothing else.

In economics, the term consumerism refers to economic policies that encourage consumption. In a consumerist society, people are bombarded by adverts, discounts, product launches, and product giveaways, among many other promotions. The prime objective is to encourage constant and significant spending on goods and services. Before proceeding to the pros and cons, let me ask you to do a simple task.

Check your wardrobe and take out a shirt or a saree and recollect how many times you have worn it. I am sure none of us would cross five. Why? Because before the existing dress could wear off, we have bought a dozen new clothes to follow the latest trend. As the trend changes, our demands rise to the next level. Coming to think of it, over-consumption has become the newest trend without us realizing its harmful consequences.

Let us have a quick look at the benefits of consumerism.

- Economic growth: Consumerism drives economic growth. When people spend more on goods/services produced in a never-ending cycle, the economy grows. There is increased production and employment, which leads to more consumption. People's living standards are also bound to improve due to consumerism.

- Paves path to innovation: Since consumers are actively looking for the next-best products/services to buy, producers/manufacturers are under constant pressure to innovate. Consequently, consumers access better goods/services, improving their living standards.

Amidst all the goodness, where does consumerism hurt?

- Environmental degradation: Increasing demand for goods puts extensive pressure on natural resources such as water and raw materials, increasing the water footprint. Excessive energy use for the increased production cycle and the generation of chemical waste degrades the environment. In a nutshell, consumerism does more harm than good to the environment.
- Moral degradation: Increasing consumerism shifted the mindset to single-use and throw. As we ape the trend, our focus gets aligned with materialism and competition. People tend to buy goods and services they don't need to be at par or a higher level than everyone else.
- Higher debt levels: Consumerism also increases debt levels in society. The number of people taking short-term loans such as payday loans to buy luxury goods has increased drastically. Many short-term loans aren't channeled into constructive use today.
- Mental health problems: It is a vicious cycle linked with financial debts. Consumerism forces people to work harder, borrow more and spend less time with loved ones. Consumerism gets in the way of fruitful relationships. It negatively affects people's overall well-being in the long run since research has proven that people don't get valuable and long-lasting fulfillment from materialism.

Humans have indulged in buying things we don't need with the money which can be saved or put to better use. Human life has a scope to improve dramatically once this pursuit of over-consumerism is removed. Businesses use advertising and marketing tactics in this modern world and encourage us to buy things we didn't even know we wanted. It is common now to buy our identities, values, and way to happiness, and in the process, we tend to forget what we are leaving behind.

> *"The attitude inherent in consumerism is that of swallowing the whole world. The consumer is the eternal suckling crying for the bottle."*
> –Erich Fromm

Let us do a little fact check here. William Rees, an urban planner at the University of British Columbia, concluded that it requires four to six hectares of land to maintain the consumption level of the average person from a high-consumption country. It means that only 1.7 hectares of ecologically productive land was available for each person on Earth during the 90s. The production, processing, and consumption, of commodities require the extraction and use of natural resources and the creation of factories and factory complexes whose operation creates toxic byproducts. Similarly, the use of commodities themselves creates pollutants and waste. The three major factors responsible for the climate crisis are the growing population, technology, and the growing rate of consumption.

> *"Few coffee drinkers realize how little of the biomass generated at a coffee farm is consumed, or the wastefulness associated with their consumption habits."*
> — Gunter Pauli

Plan Your Sustainability Route

Can you believe that Prince Charles mends a torn blazer instead of throwing it away?

If the heir of the British Monarch can reuse, and recycle a blazer, why cannot we? The key is to unwind the value of our waste. The consumption patterns are so much a part of our lives that to change our over-consumeristic attitude would require a massive cultural overhaul. Moreover, it would certainly cause economic dislocation. A drop in demand for products may lead to economic recession or even depression, along with massive unemployment. Within the current spectrum of perpetual growth, we risk being locked into a destructive mode of development in the long run to the environment. In turn, we indirectly affect the ecological balance and also promote social discrimination.

Consumption increases the resource base to meet growth and related demands. More consumption leads to more production which promotes resource exploitation and thus induce ecological imbalance. But, how does it induce any social concern? We have to understand that production of goods is an integral part of economic growth and thus, there is always a human factor associated with it. More production reflects on more working hours and cheap labor. Plan your sustainability path, for you never know the indirect impact of this prevailing crisis.

Are You A Considerate Buyer?

Every product we purchase has an environmental footprint, from the materials used to create it to the pollution emitted during manufacturing to the packaging that ends up in landfills. So before you buy, ask yourself if you really need it.

If you do, consider buying gently used instead of new, and look for minimal packaging and shipping. Vocal for local is the latest trend. Instead of ordering some exotic fruits which need to be imported, you can of course go for something that is grown locally. What is the harm in shopping at the local stores? You have already survived in an era when there was no Amazon or Flipkart. No one is asking you to abandon your purchasing power completely. The idea is to be considerate while you shop.

Do Your Big Purchases have Environmental Benefits?

If you are in the market for a new car, look for a fuel-efficient model. You'll save thousands on petrol money and reduce your carbon footprint over the years. If you're buying a new refrigerator, washer, or dryer, look for the Energy Star label to find the most efficient appliances. Opt for a solar heater instead of an electric geyser. Sustainability is cost-effective and is profitable for the environment and your wallet.

Reduce Plastic Waste

Reuse- Reduce-Recycle may sound retro, but it is the need of the hour. Today billions of pounds of plastic can be found in swirling convergences that make up about 40 percent of the world's ocean surfaces. Every year thousands of seabirds, sea turtles, seals, and other marine mammals are killed after ingesting plastic or getting tangled up in it. Honestly, plastic is a wonderful invention by humans. So, if we cannot reduce its usage any further, we can certainly increase the longevity of the product instead of discarding.

Has Your Product Endangered Wildlife?

Whether you are wearing a mink coat or setting up an industry by cutting down a forest, you are the culprit in damaging the ecosystem.

Are You Trying to Grow Anything Exotic?

Let us understand, nature has its own way of nurturing foods. There is a reason why tropical fruits grow in a particular region. Nineteen million tons of carbon dioxide are released into the atmosphere by transport used to import food. Moreover, trying to produce something that is not an inherent fauna needs more resources than expected while raising the water footprint.

Are You Water Wise?

Bottled water companies try to give tap water a bad name, even though the tap water is practically free and much of the city water has won quality tests against brand-name water. The extraction of water and production of plastic bottles is also notoriously harmful to communities and wildlife. Water conservation is also critical, especially as our growing population puts increased demand on the nation's water resources, and we face unprecedented droughts.

Kicking Out The Fossil Fuel Is Good

Kicking the fossil fuel habit is critical to saving wildlife, slowing climate change, and protecting our lands and waters. If your locality has a Green-electricity certified company that generates at least half its power from wind, solar, and other clean sources, opt for that. Many houses in India are now installing rooftop solar panels or solar water heating.

Do you wish to make anyone extinct?

Meat production and processing have many leaky faucets. Go green, not only in your vehicles but also on your food plate.

Make A Sustainable Population

Parenting is blissful, but overpopulation is creating a dread worldwide. We can achieve an ecologically sustainable population in ways that promote human rights; decrease poverty and overcrowding; raise our standard of living; and allow plants, animals, and ecosystems to thrive. It is time to talk about the runaway human population growth, the extinction crisis looming over many species, and what kind of future we want for wildlife, the planet, and ourselves.

Sustainability at a Larger Platform

Considering climate change is a global phenomenon, sustainability programs must occupy a proper place on a bigger platform. The business councils and industries must also strategize their sustainability programs. Let us have a look at the various possible ways.

Nurture A Genuine Intention

Sustainability needs to be incorporated into corporate strategies and reflected in organizational business goals. Sustainability should be a priority in every aspect of organizational operations. As with any other business initiative, you need to make a plan of action and assign responsibility. Hold people accountable and measure the results. Keep the momentum of sustainability-agile in the organization.

Make Sustainability a Team Effort

Invest time in training employees on the importance of sustaining the environment and share what the organization is doing to help conserve resources. Encourage participation and accept additional ideas from employees for resource conservation. Most of the time, what the employees' experience can offer ideas to reduce waste and improve their work environment.

"Everything that we need for our survival and well-being depends, either directly or indirectly, on our natural environment. Sustainability creates and maintains the conditions under which humans and nature can exist in productive harmony, that permit fulfilling the social, economic, and other requirements of present and future generations. Sustainability is important to make sure that we have and will continue to have the water, materials, and resources to protect human health and our environment."
    – Environment Protection Agency (U.S.A.)

Keep a watch on Water Footprint

The water footprint of an individual, community, or business is defined as the total volume of fresh water used to produce the goods and services consumed by the individual or community or produced by the business. The more robust approach is for businesses to go beyond simple volumetric measurement to assess the full range of water impact from all sites. The organization must hold accounts on water availability, water quality, health impacts, and operating licenses. We can all participate in conserving our water by reducing the opportunities for wasting this valuable resource.

How Compliant Is Your Supply Chain?

Do you have a vendor who understands the gravity of the situation? If your supplier is not compliant with sustainability benefits and approaches, your business will share their carbon/water footprint. Let us consider a scenario where you run a textile factory and outsource the dye. Your supplier of dyes is one of the best in the market regarding the quality of the dye; however, have you checked about his waste disposal method? What if your supplier releases untreated effluents into the environment? While you try to comply with the environmental protection mindset, your supplier is not. And as you encourage this business relationship to prosper, you indirectly let your supplier keep making the same mistake. The present situation of worsening climate demands closer scrutiny of every ingredient in the production cycle.

Develop a Recycling Program

Encourage an in-house program for recyclable products like fluorescent lightbulbs, electronics, computers and monitors, plastic recycling, and paper products. Work with a waste management company to chalk out a better recycling plant.

If you are a manufacturer of plastic buckets and other plastic items, you can always work in close association with organizations that work in plastic recycling.

Manage The Use Of Chemicals

Chemistry and chemicals form an integral part of inventions, manufacturing cycles and growth. We cannot abandon the use of chemicals but can always switch to the least harmful ones. Also, work out a plan to dispose of the wastes without harming the environment. Leaving your industrial waste untreated and letting it out into the environment is a crime as serious as committing murder. How? Your waste is like a slow poison to Mother Earth.

Every government around the world has become vocal about waste treatment before disposal. Start a Sustainability Policy at the Workplace. It is better to develop sustainability policies and procedures to reinforce the efforts. Things like powering down equipment at the end of the day and enabling energy savings settings on all computers and desktops are examples of policies that can support the cause.

> *"If you really think economy is more important than environment, try holding your breath whilst counting money."*
> – Dr. Guy McPherson

As an environmental engineer, let me give you **15 Quick Mantras** to build an immediate aid in escaping the climate change.

> ➤ *Pre-set your AC and Geyser limits* – It reduces power consumption and in turn you pay less and save more.
> ➤ *Prefer air-coolers over an AC* – Less power consumption and less pollution.
> ➤ *Use five star rated electrical appliances* – They are environment friendly.
> ➤ *Avoid single usage of car to reduce fuel consumption.*

➢ *Be comfortable using Public Transport.*

➢ *Restrict air-travel* – Keep it as an emergency exit for it saves a lot on carbon footprint.

➢ *Using solar panels for heating* – It reduces power consumption and in turn reduces the need of power generation.

➢ *Encourage the use of Auto-switches* – Illumination is the greatest guzzler of electricity. Auto-switches may poke us for the initial costs but are beneficial on the long run.

➢ *Avoid Single Use Plastic Bags, Bottles, etc.* – Using natural jute or other cloth bags help in negating the plastic catastrophe and also provide livelihood to the concerned workers.

➢ *Encourage re cycling of plastic, glass as well as other materials*

➢ *Opt for retreading of tyres* – It saves cost.

➢ *Avoid wood usage as much as possible at home.*

➢ *Encourage organically sourced eatables like fruits, cereals etc* – It is good for health and also reduces expenditure.

➢ *Stop food wastage at big gatherings.*

➢ *Encourage minimal menu in the social gatherings.*

The challenge to sustain the environment can be overwhelming, but if each organization, large or small, does its part, we can all contribute to conserving this great planet that we call home. Amidst the profit-oriented mindsets of the business world, we are all contributing to the crisis by sticking to our ultra-consumeristic attitude.

Much like this prevalent Corona virus, the after-effects of climate change will not differentiate between the rich and the poor.

The repercussions would be loud and visible for every human on Earth. Man destroying nature in the name of development is worse than an act of vandalism. Climate crisis needs our attention and encouraging sustainable lifestyle on personal, social, and industrial levels is the need of the hour. Chemistry and materials innovation cannot solve all our problems. We have come to a stage where people's choices matter the most.

Weighing the risks and rewards of new materials shall also accompany recognizing the potential problems regulations to combat them, willpower, collaboration, and collective action. History holds plenty of lessons; however, have we learned from the lessons?

Are The Conglomerates Playing Their Role?

The idea of globalization revolves around doing everything globally. When a business crosses borders, it kindles economic growth to different countries. The present mindset of doing business has initiated a new terminology altogether. Have you heard of Glocalization? It is about: Think Globally and Act Locally. Consider the benefits of packaged food in a country like Germany, where many houses do not have a proper kitchen.

However, in a country like India, where we are fonder of home-cooked food or mom-made food, what is the utility of packaged food? Still, the market is growing with each passing day, and several entrepreneurs have started their businesses exploiting the benefits of packaged foods. Innovative techniques improved the shelf-life and Voila! A new product is there in the market.

Walking on a similar premise, have you read Rujuta Diwekar's books? She is an Indian nutritionist who is extremely vocal about locally grown, home-cooked foods. India's weather conditions support the consumption of ghee, milk, and its products. Similarly, we can fulfill our protein requirements through Rajma, Bengal Gram, etc.; we do not need to import salmon to have a protein diet. Still, the big honchos in the market try to overdo with the benefits of exotic fruits and vegetables just to allure more and more customers.

Globalization, of course, showcases a plethora of benefits. Technology transfer, cultural influence, knowledge exchange are all vital for the growth of the human race. However, in our quest to fit into society, we have started to ape whatever others do.

In that case, we can always borrow this thinking of sustainable living and implement it locally. The scientific community and many governments have urged the bigger conglomerates to take up the initiative of sustainability as their contribution to the crisis are far more than the consumer. Large corporations have been playing a greater role in damaging the environment. Thus, it becomes imperative for them to employ sustainability. Similarly, it is important to recognize which businesses are making a positive environmental impact, and in turn, we can appreciate and support their efforts.

Apple Calls It Environment Responsibility

The tech giant has made it a mission to reduce carbon emissions and partner with companies in their supply chain that share similar values. They use mostly aluminum instead of other materials because it produces lower emissions. Moreover, twenty-three of their partners are committed to 100% renewable energy.

Apple has embarked on a new production path while manufacturing without taking from the Earth. Their innovative mindset focuses on climate change, where they take responsibility for the emissions associated with their own operations and the entire lifecycle of all our products and accessories. They try to conserve Earth's resources when operating their facilities and making their products. Moreover, they have opted for the concept of smarter chemistry as they believe that their products should be safe for anyone who assembles, uses, or recycles them. Apple takes responsibility for the entire carbon footprint emissions beyond our direct control. They work out to reduce the carbon footprint right from sourcing materials, manufacturing units, and customers using their devices. Apple calculates the carbon footprint in five major areas: corporate facilities, product manufacturing, product use, product transportation, and product end-of-life processing. This sequential process of analysis has helped them chalk out where to focus.

Apple's transition to renewable energy has reduced its Scope 1 emission from fuel consumption and Scope 2 emission by limiting the waste of electricity. Since 2011, the reduction has been up to 64%, thus preventing over 2.8 million metric tons of carbon dioxide from entering the atmosphere. Similarly, Apple has reduced plastic use in their packaging by 48% in three years. They have also started to use recycled cobalt sourced from iPhone batteries. They had launched their 2018 MacBook Air, and Mac mini with 100% recycled aluminum enclosures and cut the carbon footprint of each product nearly in half. Apple's effort to refurbish more than 7.8 million devices and recycle more than 48,000 metric tons of e-waste in 2019 has been praiseworthy. Apple supports the zero-waste ideology and is working to reuse, recycle, compost, or convert all the waste to energy in their own facilities and in and out their supply chain. The mission is big, and the journey to make the climate optimum for everyone will be long. Thus, multiple Apple teams, local governments, and specialty recyclers have come forward to work hand in hand.

"Climate change is one of the greatest threats facing our planet. Clean energy technology offers tremendous benefits to our suppliers, electricity grids, and communities around the world. We believe that if policymakers fully and properly value these benefits, clean energy becomes more cost-competitive than fossil fuel energy. Market and policy design is not one-size-fits-all, so we work closely with our suppliers and local experts to find the best solution for each country. For the past four years, we have been advocating for strong climate policies that promote decarbonizing our economy and support procurement of renewable energy."

– Lisa P. Jackson

(Apple's Vice President of Environment, Policy, and Social Initiative)

Sustainability is increasingly becoming a critical requirement for multinational corporations, often highlighted as primary contributors to unsustainable environmental and societal practices.

Do you know that more than 70% of the global greenhouse gas emissions since 1988 are from just 100 companies? Several multinational companies are vocal about sustainability; they must follow their words with real concrete and decisive action. Greenwashing has become a significant problem in which many corporates are making bold and exaggerated claims about their levels of sustainability but not doing much in reality.

IKEA is moving closer to recycling

Ikea is gradually transforming its value chain by designing its products from the start as repurposed, reused, recycled, repaired, and resold. Their motive is to generate the least possible waste. The Ikea Group is aiming towards 100% renewable energy in IKEA operations and at their direct suppliers. They are also seeking to use more sustainable product materials. By 2030, they are committed to using only recyclable and renewable materials and reducing the IKEA climate footprint by 70% per product. It is certainly encouraging to see some of the changes that multinationals are making to become more sustainable.

However, considering the gravity of our climate and environmental crises, large-scale and systemic changes need to happen across all sectors globally. Additionally, sustainable changes also need to take into account employees' livelihoods and address the issue of resource depletion and overconsumption.

Investment in sustainable education and infrastructure is crucial, and managers must be educated about environmentally responsible choices. Much like how climate change didn't happen overnight, sustainability for a year or so cannot bring in the necessary change. To make a lasting impact, the big conglomerates require a commitment to transparency and bold fundamental, systemic change. Can A Country Sustain With Sustainable Lifestyle? As we have an unquenchable attitude to accept whatever the Western Countries provide, let us prove the benefits of sustainability through a European lens.

Do you know that France has been shifting away from industrialization by focusing on environmental efforts? The French are leading the way in tackling food waste and have been named the world's most food sustainable country. As of 2016, supermarkets were required to redistribute leftover food to charities. They are cutting down on their reliance on chemical fertilizers and using more environmental-friendly options.

Currently, 30% of their energy is generated from renewable sources, and they plan on increasing that percentage. In addition, they also plan on phasing out cars running on diesel to reduce particle pollution. Is it not an impactful action to protect and preserve the environment?

Swedish inventors have been developing new technologies to run on 100% renewable energy and recycled sources. Passive houses are on the go to reduce energy consumption by using heat energy from human activities and Sunlight. Stockholm's Central Station captures body heat from daily commuters. This concept is also used in district heating for blocks of apartment buildings. Public transport runs on biogas and renewable energy, while cycling is encouraged. Similarly, in the land of chocolate and cheese, Switzerland is a leader in the world of sustainability. Waste and recycling management are prioritized as waste is properly disposed of, turning the rest into energy. Most of the power is hydroelectrically generated, which lowers the country's overall carbon footprint. They preserve water quality and biodiversity by protecting land and designating these lots as National Parks.

Is India Doing Enough?

Considering the growing number of industries and MNCs choosing India as their innovation hub, several big honchos are working out on their sustainability programs as a part of their Corporate Social Responsibility (CSR). So, before we go into the cocoon of fear or shame, let us look at how Indian companies are playing a role in fighting this issue.

ITC's CSR unit invariably focuses on solid waste management with a Pan India prominence. In the southern states, it works with several temples towards their inventiveness of the Green Temple Project. The company's initiatives focus on creating replicable, scalable, and sustainable municipal solid waste management models that can be implemented across the country to ensure that zero waste goes to landfills.

Similarly, they work for the Soil and Moisture Conservation program, aiming to ensure water security for all dependents in the factory catchments. This initiative is to make agri-catchments drought-proof to minimize risks to agricultural livelihoods arising from drought and moisture stress. The program promotes the development and management of local water resources in moisture-stressed areas by encouraging community participation in planning and implementing such measures. They promote and help in building, reviving, and maintaining water-harvesting structures. The coverage of this program currently extends to 38 districts of 14 states. In their CSR report for the FY20-21, the area under the watershed increased by 97,549 acres, taking the cumulative coverage area to over 12.31 lakh acres.

ITC built 3,006 water-harvesting structures, creating 3.94 million cubic meters of rainwater harvesting potential. Additionally, as a part of their sustainability program, the company continues to work with farmers to achieve 'more crop per drop' by promoting agronomic practices and micro-irrigation techniques. It helps in saving water in cultivation and improving farmer incomes. Around three lakh acres have been covered to date across six states.

Similarly, REC Limited works in collaboration with Andhra Pradesh State Biodiversity Board, Madurai Kamaraj University, New & Renewable Energy Development Corporation of Andhra Pradesh, District Magistrate, Solar Energy Corporation of India, Social Work and Research Centre, IIM Tiruchirappalli, Karnataka Residential Educational Institutions Society and Punjab University. Indian Oil has set up a 100 tons per day cattle dung-based Biogas plant at Jaipur, Rajasthan.

Under the sponsorship of the Swachh Bharat Mission of the Govt. of India the installation of a Biogas plant has provided the option for procuring clean energy for cooking and other purposes and yield better quality manure. It is an attempt in the spectrum of Make in India and Swachh Bharat's mission.

Regarding energy generation, although India is looking forward to renewable sources of energy to combat pollution and excess resource exploitation, there are various constraints. Our groaning about pollution does not make any significant change besides creating pollution; our unbridled consumption patterns have put us into a disadvantageous position. We have to understand that the wrath of nature spreads over everything. An industry may be located in the US, but the pollution caused by it is shared by every ingredient in the demand and supply chain. Climate crisis doesn't know the political boundaries as pollution at one place expands to its overall kitty and affects other domains too.

Do you remember the Chernobyl Nuclear accident? If you watch the web series Chernobyl, you will realize how man is the destroyer of his own destiny. The nuclear power plant accident occurred at Chernobyl. Still, its malignant and toxic effects were felt in the air, land, and water in carrying the disaster to faraway countries like France, Sweden, and other Nordic countries. The climate crisis is an all-encompassing issue transcending countries, continents, and oceans. Damage done at one place will soon be felt everywhere due to a chain reaction.

On the other hand, India has continuously acknowledged the emerging threats from climate change and implemented some actions. We have been working on the principles of improving the efficiency of the economy while using sustainability as our engine of growth. India has been actively promoting clean energy and clean technology while continuing the flagship schemes on combating climate change through adaptation and mitigation. As a developing country, we have to understand that efficient utilization of resources is the key to a growing population. Our urge to get a hand on everything increases the demand for resources.

For implementing a better lifestyle, at both personal and global levels, the government must come forward with policies to nudge economic growth in an Earth-friendly way. However, it becomes pertinent that unless every individual understands the gravity of the problem and reorient himself towards a changed mindset and lifestyle, no governmental policies can help us. The goal is global; thus, the players must come forward from every stratum of society, be it government bodies, private organizations, or people at large. And here, the conundrum beats at the bottom level where every citizen has a role to play in combating the crisis.

Thus, a movement on a pan-national basis is necessary to bring about the changes in our lifestyles so that the pressure on the energy, water, and material needs are minimized. But then again, is minimizing going to reduce your comfort level? Absolutely not. Reduced consumption leads to a healthier life while paving the path to success. If you hold a fresh lens to observe this perspective of a minimalistic lifestyle, you shall find yourself as a part of the solution and not the problem.

It is a crisis time indeed. However, there remains a ray of hope when we realize the significance of having a sustainable lifestyle. As I hold my lens to see the worsening situation of consumerism, lack of responsible action, I grasped one weird concept about our existence. If climate crisis is taken as evil, we have overlooked this evil before. We permitted the evil by legalizing and promoting our hunger for material goods. And then, when a handful of people tried to tell us our wrongdoings, we persecuted them to even think of climate crisis as evil.

And now, here we are, with time ticking fast; we, humans, must sprint towards sustainability to preserve Mother Earth.

"Sustainable development is development that meets the needs of the present without compromising the ability of future generations to meet their own needs."
— Gro Harlem Brundtland

PART II
A RACE WE CAN WIN

4

IS THERE A WAY OUT?

Inventions and innovations from the last century have shaped modern life for us. And believe it or not, all these luxuries come with a hidden cost. Mother Earth, the human body, the surrounding nature encompassing the motley of floras and faunas, vibrant maple trees to bleak cactus and everything narrate an unbridled tale of science. It took centuries for humans to unleash their desires towards utilizing every wonder of nature. However, in this pursuit of gaining and acquiring, utilizing got a new connotation, much similar to that of exploitation.

"The world is unrecognizable from 100 years ago, simply because of the materials that we have around, let alone all the new ways we use them."
– Anna Ploszajski

Do you know that World War I is often called The Chemist's War? At the brink of the 20th century, organic chemists learned how to turn coal into a variety of industrial chemicals like dyes and perfumes. As the war progressed, the extraordinary demands allowed the chemists to hone their craft with poison gas.

Explosives, propellants, disinfectants, and antibiotics came into play. Material science has been like a parent to humans' comfort and convenience in the last century. Humans walked from stone to bronze and from bronze to iron.

The journey was revolutionary but relatively slow in terms of the time scale. The changes in materials innovation and application within the last half-century occurred in a time span that is revolutionary rather than evolutionary. Through basic curiosity and coincidence, many new materials took birth in humanity. With every new invention, a door to innovation was opened. Presently, humans are capable of designing materials from scratch to solve specific problems. Humanity's constant exploration of various natural resources, their interactions with heat, light, electricity, or magnetism helped iterate new products. From CD and floppy discs, we are handed over memory chips.

While studying how matter interacts with biological tissues, humans went ahead in developing coronary stents, artificial skin, hip replacements, and many other medical marvels. Polymer science led to one of the most wondrous creations of humans: plastic. Malleable, ductile, reusable and reshaped; our lives are entangled with the benefits of plastics.

We have come a long way from the days of celluloid and Bakelite. Tens of thousands of plastic compounds exist today. The world now produces in excess of 380 million metric tons of plastic a year. But then, every innovation comes with consequences. With each story of progress, a tale of alteration in the natural balance persists. While enabling humans to flourish, many new substances have become pollutants, from PCBs to plastics.

However, when people go about addressing these environmental problems, other new materials will likely be part of the solutions. With hundreds of industrial inventions by our side, humans cannot unmake the stuff that have been created. But can we not recycle them or increase the product's lifecycle? Instead of enjoying the use and throw system, can we not encourage the concept of reusing and recycling?

Enhance The Lifecycle Of Every Product

The annals of human history will be adorned with the advances of science and development; however, the same records will also narrate humans claim to have a toxic love story between humans and the products invented.

Let us consider this example. When we use plastics regularly, we nurture nothing less than a toxic love story even after knowing about the plethora of plastic wastes. Every new product that comes into the market carries a set lifecycle, whether it is a new mobile phone or a new fashion trend. While innovation has reached a new crescendo, every product faces a shortened life, which adds an extra burden on the amount of waste generated. Consider the lifecycle of a simple cotton dress material. We receive the final product at our hands; however, the product lifecycle begins right from the node of cotton production. Water used, land plowed, fertilizers or manure produced and utilized to support the plantation followed by the harvest forms the first stage in the lifecycle. Similarly, the manpower involved, machines included in the production of the dress, brand management, supply-chain management, operational units and everything come under the purview of a simple cotton dress material.

Every product that is placed on your hand undergoes a series of processing, involving different factors and components, which invariably leaves a mark on the carbon footprint and water footprint. As John Muir quoted– When we try to pick out anything by itself, we find it hitched to everything else in the Universe.

Today, as climate change has become the new normal, we must understand how every step we take as a human is interlinked with its own set of pros and cons. Let me put it in simple words. We need water to drink and raise plants that provide us with food and other essential products to live. The same water is required in order to run a factory; whether in the power generation or during the operational process.

And then again, if we are going to dispose of our waste into the same water bodies, we are just reducing our chances to acquire water for our essential purposes. The concept of production and waste generation runs through a vicious, inescapable cycle. Every product has a set lifespan, and invariably it would end in the dump yard. However, as the climate crisis is growing faster, we must consider the resources used in the production process before throwing away any product.

Before you change your phone, ask if it is necessary? Before you throw away a plastic bucket as waste, just recalculate if the bucket can be reused for any other purpose if not bathing. We cannot deny that this whole concept of production, manufacturing, and even waste disposal constitutes a big economy and the whole world earns its bread through this. We can neither stop the process of innovation nor can we deny the advantages of these products. However, we can always try to increase the lifecycle of every product we use. If a product crosses its lifespan, just pause and ponder if it can be recycled again for a different purpose. We can never forget that the economy is embedded within society and the environment.

The most common sense relates economy to a process: society uses natural resources to create products and services that people need or want, e.g., homes for shelter and food for nourishment. Our economy, society, and environment are interdependent systems - the vitality of one affects the vitality of them all. This is the simple yet profound reality that begins our understanding of systems. The economy cannot grow irreconcilably without adversely affecting the society and environment.

"If it can't be reduced, reused, repaired, rebuilt, refurbished, resold, recycled, or composted, then it should be restricted, redesigned or removed from production."
– Pete Seeger

Have you heard of Patagonia's Worn Wear program?

It encourages product life extension through the repair and reuse of Patagonia and non-Patagonia products. In 2017, Patagonia launched an online store where customers trade-in their used clothing in return for store credit and can buy previously-owned Patagonia gear at a lower price point and give it a second life.

All second-hand products are covered by their ironclad guarantee, ensuring strict quality standards. The company repaired 30,000 products in the first 18 months after the launch of their campaign and sold used clothes worth $1mn in the first six months of the launch of the website.

Linear Economy: A Frankenstein's Monster

Humanity has gone through evolution, diversification, and even globalization, and amid all this, the fundamental characteristic of the industrial revolution remains unaltered. We still cling onto the linear model of resource consumption that revolves around the take-make-dispose pattern. Industries extract materials, apply energy and workforce to manufacture a product and sell it to an end consumer who discards it as soon as it no longer serves its purpose. While we strive to improve resource efficiency, a system that is based on consumption rather than on the restorative use of resources demands significant losses throughout the value chain.

This linear economy system increases exposure to risks of higher resource prices as the resources are exhaustible. Almost every form of business feels squeezed between rising and unpredictable costs of the resources. Moreover, as the consumers are slowly getting acquainted with the climate problem, there grows a stagnation in demand.

The dawn of the 21st century had witnessed the turning point when real prices of natural resources surged uncontrollably. The cost of metals, food, and non-food agricultural products has become atrociously volatile with the growing population and urbanization. Resource extraction has metamorphosed into resource exploitation.

Human activities and the employed economic model have been working on the principle of extraction and depletion. Consecutively, the vital equilibrium that exists between the economy, society, and environment has been diminished. Although we think a lot about reusing or recycling, we still cling to a linear economy.

It is equivalent to consuming the earth's finite natural resources, leading to high levels of waste and pollution that threaten the biosphere and human health. About two billion people continue to exist in basic agrarian conditions or worse in the present era. At the same time, three billion are expected to join the ranks of middle-class consumers by 2030. What will be the outcome of this new prosperity? It will certainly trigger a surge of demand both greater and in a shorter period than the world has ever experienced before. Even the most conservative prognoses for global economic growth over the next decade suggest that demand for oil, coal, iron ore, and other natural resources will rise by at least a third, with about 90% of that increase coming from growth in emerging markets. Basically, as we fail to see the economic, social, and environmental spheres as intimately connected, we perpetually miss the bus and continue to undermine our chances of future prosperity.

The premise of the linear economy is simple; however, it leaves a convoluted impact on the Earth's climate. The linear production model incurs unnecessary resource losses in several ways. There is significant waste in the production chain itself. In producing goods, significant volumes of materials are commonly lost in the chain between resource extraction and final manufacturing. Some materials never enter the economic system, such as overburden and parting materials from mining, by-catch from fishing, wood, agricultural harvesting losses, and soil excavation and dredged materials from construction activities

The food markets exhibit the best snapshot of wastage along the value chain. Losses of materials occur at different steps like losses in the field due to pests or pathogens, losses during agricultural production due to poor efficiency, spills or leakages during transport amid the global export of exotic foods.

And then, losses happen during storage and at the retailers due to food surpassing its sell-by date and going unused by end consumers. These global losses add up to an estimated one-third of food produced for human consumption every year along the entire food supply chain.

We have a time-crunch, and if we wish to find our way out, we need to think differently. Consider the human world as a machine. Every part must be thoroughly scrutinized to make it work efficiently and effectively. If climate change is the problem, we must disentangle every aspect of it before applying the principle of reductionism.

A linear economy is neither predictable nor understandable. It is completely mechanized – resources go in, and waste comes out. It is like a conveyer belt, continuously moving with the primary goal to increase efficiency and drive endless economic growth. A linear economy is an example of an abstracted economy, entirely divorced from any connection to the broader natural and social systems that maintain it. To be precise, a linear economy traditionally follows the "take-make-dispose" step-by-step plan. The raw materials are collected then transformed into products that are used until they are finally discarded as waste. Value is created in this economic system by producing and selling as many products as possible.

The only way out is by introducing the concept of systems thinking to understand how the parts of a system interact to produce the behavior of the whole. We get the freedom to identify the root causes of problems and see new opportunities through system thinking. At the opposite end of the spectrum, if we keep struggling with the same linear economic model, we shall produce more and more Frankenstein's monsters. If you see through the business models of various business houses, you will find two fangs for their monstrous tactics while dealing with manufacturing electronic gadgets or appliances. Let's say that an appliance finishes every scope of its utility, and the product reaches the brink of its endpoint. It does have a chance to get repaired, but that is denied. To enhance sales report, there prevails a standard reply.

Every salesperson is instructed to parrot out the same word – irreparable; buy the latest one. The business world is flourishing more because of our use and throw policy. The whopping waste we generate is actually contributing to their success and, on the other hand, failing nature. Do you remember that Nokia 1100 mobile phone?

Almost every one of us would have used this phone. Do you remember the longevity and scope of repairing? Nokia and Apple mobile phones have some contrasting features to ponder upon. Each part of Nokia phones can be separated and repaired separately. The consumers themselves can change the battery. On the other hand, Apple phones' batteries cannot be touched, leaving aside internal repairs. The concept of repairing was available for the line of computers, that too to some extent only. A couple of years later, even that was stopped. Even if repaired, the costs are so prohibitive that the consumer would prefer to go for the new one. Such organizations bring out new products on an iterative basis every year with huge marketing budgets and few updates. Nevertheless, the product would be touted as flagship and flagship killer models. The peer pressure is so huge on the gullible consumer that he would invest in the new one even at the cost of his heirlooms. The old one would be relegated to someone down the pecking order, and it would go to the dust bin in no time.

Today, electronics waste is a monstrous problem. With each passing year, the burden of electronic waste is growing by leaps and bounds. The job of combatting the waste is usually outsourced to the third world, where the statutory requirements are quite loose and with no governmental oversight. These waste handling units work under questionable premises with unhealthy practices, thereby leading to leakage into the atmosphere. The incineration process produces poisonous gases too. The truth behind prospering business stands naked now, and the world has awakened by the hue and cry made by the green brigade. Big MNCs like Apple have now seriously shifted their focus on making all their products repairable to some extent.

So, where can we commoners play a role in the process? As responsible citizens, we must choose only those gadgets and appliances where reparability is possible. Our small attempt shall reduce the piling up of electronic wastes and e-hazards. Factually, the consumer is indeed God. Pressure from the consumers is much more effective than government-imposed rules and regulations.

This bottom-up approach remains the best route to achieve a speedy result. The linear 'take-make-dispose' model relies on large quantities of easily accessible resources and energy. It is increasingly unfit for the reality of the climate crisis within which it operates. Working towards efficiency alone, i.e., reducing resources and fossil energy consumed per unit of manufacturing output, will not alter the limited stock but shall positively delay the inevitable. A change of the entire operating system has become a dire necessity.

"The ultimate test of man's conscience may be his willingness to sacrifice something today for future generations whose words of thanks will not be heard."
—Gaylord Nelson

The Ray of Hope: Circular Economy

Sustainable living has a deeper root in the mindset. Acting towards sustainable development requires disruptive changes in the way our societies and businesses are organized. The ideology of circular economy opens the door to innovation. Integrating natural ecosystems, businesses, our daily lives, and waste management has become the need of the hour for our sustenance.

A circular economy model aims to close the gap between the production and the natural ecosystems' cycles on which humans ultimately depend upon. On the one hand, the motive is to eliminate waste, composting biodegradable waste or, in the case of non-biodegradable wastes, circular economy emphasizes reusing, remanufacturing, and finally recycling.

Similarly, another leaflet of circular economy advocates for the use and implementation of renewable energy. A circular economy is an industrial system that is restorative or regenerative by intention and design. It replaces the end-of-life concept with restoration, shifts towards the use of renewable energy, and eliminates the use of toxic chemicals.

A circular economy aims to eliminate waste through the superior design of materials, products, systems, and business models. It redefines growth while focusing on positive society-wide benefits. Implementing a circular economy is an effort to decouple economic activities from the consumption of finite resources. And with every scientific and socialistic community supporting the principles of circular economy, it is the most fruitful way to build economic, natural, and social capital.

The concept of the circular economy is stranded in the study of non-linear systems like the living systems. It borrows the notion of optimizing systems rather than components, which can also be referred to as 'design to fit.' It involves careful management of material flows and focuses on biological nutrients returning to the biosphere safely and building natural capital. Similarly, a circular economy demands technical nutrients to circulate at high quality without entering the biosphere. A circular economy advocates the need for a functional model in which manufacturers or retailers increasingly retain the ownership of their products and act as service providers. This shift has direct implications for developing efficient and effective take-back systems and the proliferation of designing durable products. The intention is to facilitate disassembly and refurbishment and consider product/service shifts.

"The linear model turned services into products that can be sold, but this throughput approach is a wasteful one. In the past, reuse and service-life extension were often strategies in situations of scarcity or poverty and led to products of inferior quality. Today, they are signs of good resource husbandry and smart management."
– Walter Stahel

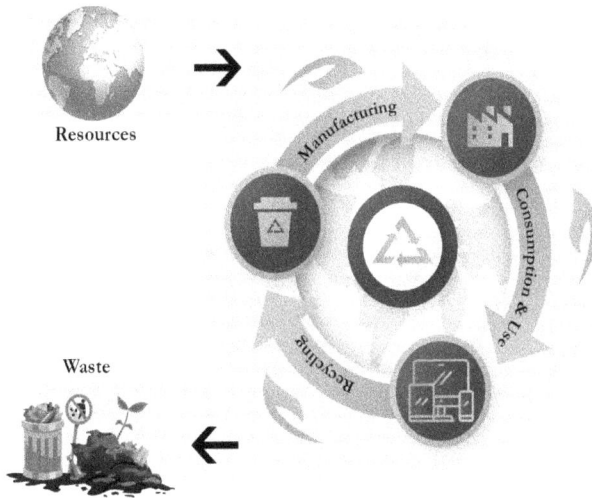

As we can realize from this picture, the circular economy is an economic system of closed loops in which raw materials, components, and products lose their value as little as possible while using renewable energy sources. We all should come together in transforming every element of our take-make-waste system. Analyze how we manage resources, how we make and use products, and what we do with the materials afterward. These are some of the essential points to consider before creating a thriving circular economy that can benefit everyone within the limits of our planet.

The circular economy can be represented as the tool to tackle climate change and biodiversity loss together while addressing important social needs. On the same note, it also bestows us with the power to grow prosperity, jobs, and resilience while cutting greenhouse gas emissions, waste, and pollution. Sustainable living while encouraging a circular economy not only reduces the burden on Mother Earth but also adds money to our wallets.

Is Circular Economy The Key To Fight Climate Change?

Mother Earth was a balanced and healthy planet functioning in a completely circular way. Before humans, the idea of trash never existed. Moreover, a balanced ecosystem will not have the slightest inkling of the word waste. A flower blooms, ages, and dies, and soon is decomposed by the natural microbes in nature. If we look at the natural processes, we shall find that nature has its own way to reap benefits from waste. Dinosaurs died and got buried and formed fossil fuels. Similarly, if we study the decomposers of the food chain, waste of one level is always the food for another level.

Since the first industrial revolution, humankind has been following a linear approach regarding how we use natural resources. In our quest for modernity, we have demonstrated considerable ignorance concerning the impact of our inventions. In our chain reaction of extracting, transforming, manufacturing, using and discarding resources, we have come a long way.

While we read so much about the circular economy, can you believe that it is only followed by 9% of the world today? It essentially implies that only 9% of 92.8 billion tons of minerals, metals, biomass, and fossil fuels that enter the economy are re-used every year. And the remaining 91% is tagged as a circular gap. The global economy is heading in the worst direction, misguided to the core while making money through ultra-consumerism.

Closing the circular gap can serve as a fundamental step in fighting climate change, but for that, society must endorse the change. The circular economy dictates a different outlook. By improving the resource efficiency, greenhouse gases can be reduced.

Adopt the principles like re-using, re-manufacturing or recycling. Not only at the personal level, but the world's supply chains should be re-engineered to go all the way back to the wells, fields, mines, and quarries where our resources originate. A reduction in GHG makes a more efficient economy. Presently, most concerned citizens and communities plan to fight climate change by focusing on stopping deforestation and encouraging the use of renewable energy.

Similarly, the concept of biodegradable plastic is also encouraged. However, circular rekindles our hope by planning to reduce the amount of waste itself. There is indeed a world of opportunity to re-think and re-design the way we make and use our products. The idea is to implant a changed perspective to re-design the way our economy works.

Science is like a magic wand for us. Should we not indulge in designing products that can be 'made to be made again'? Humans carry an unfathomable ocean of curiosity and creativity. The way to combat climate change lies in our ability to build a restorative economy.

Eliminate the concept of waste from your life. The generation of waste and pollution reflects a flaw in our process design. Think of an alternative. Circulation of products and materials is crucial. Consider the reusability factor of plastic before leaving it on the landfill or shouting for biodegradable plastics. The non-biodegradable stuff is both boon and bane. Rethink over the boon part of it. Regenerate nature. Renew a sustainable lifestyle.

A circular economy is more than just recycling. It is one of the best approaches to not only combat the overenthusiastic consumption rate of the present generation but also to give a better ambiance to Earth.

"The Circular Economy is a blueprint for a new sustainable economy, one that has innovation and efficiency at its heart and addresses the business challenges presented by continued economic unpredictability, exponential population growth and our escalating demand for the world's natural resources. It presents an opportunity to fundamentally rethink how we run our business and challenge all aspects of traditional operating models, from how we use natural resources, to the way we design and manufacture products, through to how we educate and train the next generation."

– Chris Dedicoat

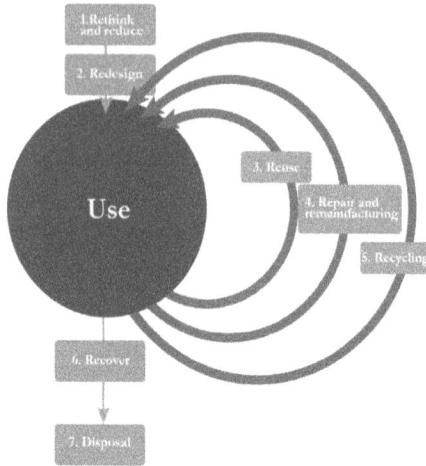

More than anything, adopting an eco-friendly mindset brings along the potential of saving money. Fixing what is temporarily broken and re-using it to participating in recycling systems is rewarding. From zero waste strategies that allow saving energy and time to minimalism behaviors, we can translate waste into more tidiness and innovation.

Impact Of Circular Economy On The Environment

One of the goals of the circular economy is to have a positive effect on the planet's ecosystems and to fight the excessive exploitation of natural resources. The circular economy has the potential to reduce greenhouse gas emissions and the use of raw materials, optimize agricultural productivity and decrease the negative consequences of the linear model.

Reduction in Green House Gas: Circular Economy emphasizes the use of renewable energy, which is less polluting than fossil fuels. With the idea of reusing and dematerializing, there is a considerable reduction in the need for materials and production processes. Moreover, since the preferred choices are energy-efficient and non-toxic materials, pollution is further reduced.

Resilient Soil Structure: The principles of the circular economy on the farming system ensure that important nutrients are returned to the soil through anaerobic processes or composting. It definitely softens the exploitation of land and natural ecosystems. According to a case study conducted by Ellen Macarthur Foundation, a circular economy model working in Europe's food systems has the potential to decrease 80% of the use of artificial fertilizer and therefore contribute to the natural balance of soils.

Economic Growth without affecting Mother Earth: It is a sheer necessity to decouple economic growth from resource consumption. The increase in revenues from new circular activities and cheaper production by getting products and materials more functional and easily disassembled and reused can improve the economic structure.

Resources saved: When compared with the raw material extraction in the linear approach, the circular economy model has the potential to lead to 70% amount of material savings. In the future, the total demand for materials will increase due to the growth of the world population and middle classes. A circular economy leads to lower material needs, as it skips landfills and avoids recycling, focusing on making materials' cycles last longer. Moreover, it also avoids the problems caused by excessive mining.

Job creation: With the concept of recycling and planning for sustainability programs, innovation is always round the corner. There are several small scale enterprises that run on their recycling business and in turn create jobs.

Profit-making business: Lower input cost creates entirely new profit streams for the businesses that move to the circular economy model. In this circular sphere, profit opportunities may come from playing in new markets, cutting costs off with waste and energy reductions, and the assurance of continuity of supply.

A circular economy designs out waste. As the biological and technical components of a product are designed with the intention to fit within a biological or technological materials cycle, waste doesn't exist. The product is designed for disassembly and refurbishment.

The biological nutrients are non-toxic and can be simply composted. While technical nutrients like polymers, alloys, and other man-made materials are designed to be used again with minimal energy and highest quality retention. Modularity, versatility, and adaptability are prized features of a circular economy, and thus, circular economy should be prioritized in an uncertain and fast-evolving world. It propagates resilience through diversity. Diverse systems with many connections and scales are more resilient than systems built simply for efficiency.

Natural systems of Earth support resilient abundance, for they adapt to their environments with a vast blend of diversity, uniformity, and complexity. As the industrial revolution and globalization have been focused on uniformity only, the system has been unstable. We must fix that by manufacturing products with the same flair for resilience by using successful natural systems as the model. A circular economy watches the whole system. It emphasizes flow and connection over time and has the potential to encompass regenerative conditions. The ability to reintroduce products and materials back into the biosphere through non-toxic, restorative loops forms the crux of the circular economy. And the non-biological components are sent to be upcycled.

There is a drive to shift the material composition of consumables from technical towards biological nutrients while having those cascade through different applications before extracting valuable feedstock. The idea is to restore what has been lost. Implementing a circular economic model shall provide several benefits for the environment, economy, and businesses; however, unfortunately, the concept hasn't yet received the momentum and commitment it requires.

Let us have a look at some of the major barriers to the implementation of the circular economy. The fact that our current economic system is geared towards the demand of the linear economy and is not yet prepared to deal with circular economy entrepreneurs. Legal regulations still prevail in the decision-making. No business can prosper as an island.

Plenty of businesses relies on old alliances, making it harder to create new alliances and close loops. The idea of short-term value creation is the biggest hindrance to a circular economy. The GDP index doesn't consider social and environmental externalities, discouraging the creation of value in both these areas.

"If coal plants release mercury—and mercury is a neurotoxin that damages children's brains—then reducing the amount of mercury in emissions doesn't stop that. It just says, "We'll tell you at what rate you can dispense death."
– William Mcdonough

We must remember that every new implementation takes time to get accepted, adjusted, and accommodated. After all, it took humanity 5000 years to bring in automobiles. The circular economy concept has deep-rooted origins in the past of human evolution. However, its practical applications to modern economic systems and industrial processes have gained momentum since the late 1970s as the green brigade started voicing out the impact of demand and supply chain on the climate crisis.

To date, the whole production and consumption system has spoken about eco-efficiency. It begins with the linear flow of materials through industrial systems: raw materials are extracted from the environment, transformed into products, and eventually disposed of. The eco-efficient techniques aim to minimize the volume, velocity, and toxicity of the material flow system. But does it alter the linear progression? No. Some materials are recycled as an end-of-pipe solution with quality drastically lowered, making it a process of down-cycling. The usability is limited, and it portrays the true picture of a cradle-to-grave situation.

In contrast, circular economy speaks for eco-effectiveness. It proposes the transformation of products and their associated material flows such that they form a supportive relationship with ecological systems and future economic growth. It tactfully eliminates the cradle-to-grave flow of materials while generating cyclical, cradle-to-cradle processes.

This in turn enable materials to maintain usability. Upcycling inherently generates a symbiotic relationship between ecological and economic systems. A circular economy ensures a positive recoupling of the relationship between human economy and ecology and paves the path for humans' transformation from being a parasite on Mother Earth.

Is India Looking Forward To Circular Economy?

Every economy falter at the demand and supply chain. With greater urbanization in India, there is a greater generation of waste. After all, a man staying on the 25th floor of a condominium is not able to use his bio-degradable waste as manure. With industries flourishing at the bank of rivers, Ganga, Yamuna has fallen prey to extreme degradation. Can we forget how Narendra Modi exclaimed on his Namami Gange initiative?

India is experiencing environmental degradation in extreme measures, and we have come to a stage where we must glower at our production process. Looking at waste as a by-product or even nutrients in a different form, we shall probably find a better way to use the waste instead of disposing of it. Sooner or later, circular economy practices are going to come into the mainstream.

India has an enormous opportunity for a circular economy. While carrying a fresher perspective towards prioritizing the need for resources, several organizations are switching to processes that leave a lesser environmental footprint. There is no standard model to apply for the circular economy initiative. But there are some routes we must visit at an organizational level.

Do you know that one can recover 1 billion dollars from the e-waste generated in India? Proper management of plastic waste in India can create 14 lakhs jobs. Around 8 million tons of steel can be recovered from abandoned vehicles in India. From an implementation perspective, there is a need for an enabling ecosystem that can foster the spirit of disruption and innovation.

As we understand, there is a strong correlation between the resource intensity and economic growth of any country. Emerging economies like India may not prosper if they cling to the traditional model of growth as the natural resources are already exhausted. Mother Earth had a threshold rate to provide us, and we have crossed the limit. There is a reason behind tagging a day as Earth Overshoot Day.

How To Accelerate Circular Economy?

The first step to bringing in a change is by spreading awareness. Better consumer awareness helps the commoners understand the problems. Similarly, educating entrepreneurs, designers, engineers, procurement officers, and product managers is a necessary step to make everyone understand the concept and its benefits. Climate change is a major concern for the future generation; therefore, the idea of a circular economy must be integrated into the academic curriculum itself.

The second vital step is to inculcate disruptive technology. Enabling cleaner resources, extending the lifecycle of every product, and encouraging a shared platform are good options. We should incline more towards the use of bio-based material. Honestly, humans avoid change and feel better in the cocoon of normalcy. If the policies change their landscape towards the benefits of a circular economy, a behavioral change cannot remain far behind. India has implemented some of the policies like Zero Defect-Zero Effect scheme, plastic waste recycling, and e-waste management within the scope of Circular Economy.

There are five different models to incorporate a circular economy in a mainstream organization. Several globally renowned companies have installed one of these strategies to regularize circular economy in their mode of function. At present, there are five key prospects to implementing a circular economy. And many organizations have employed one or more system in conjunction to utilize the concept of circular economy.

- Circular Supply Chain: This strategy speaks for providing renewable energy to run the production cycle. Moreover, the input material for any product should be bio-based or fully recyclable. The idea is to replace the single-use products completely.

- Recovery and Recycling: In this process, the idea is to recover resources from the disposed waste or the by-products of the production cycle.

- Product Life Extension: This principle speaks for repairing, upgrading, and recycling to extend the working lifecycle of a product or its components.

- Sharing Platform: The core focus is to increase the utilization rate of any product by making possible shared use or access or ownership.

- Product as a Service: This offers product access to consumers while retaining ownership to internalize the benefits of circular resource productivity.

Various organizations around the globe have been implementing different strategies to promote a circular economy. They are setting an example not only for their competitors but also for the commoners to consider.

BASF, the world's largest chemical producer, has integrated the Circular Supply Chain model by replacing finite fossil resources with sustainably produced renewable resources through its innovative Verbund Biomass Balance approach. The production Verbund is a set of six BASF sites globally with intelligently networked production facilities, energy flow, logistics, and infrastructure.

They maintain a closed chain of custody from renewable feedstock to the final product. According to a third-party certification, BASF has substituted 100% of fossil fuels with renewable materials in their Verbund production sites. The advancements in biological technologies and green chemistry enable organizations to identify much more sophisticated circular supply chain initiatives. The use of bio-based raw materials and biodegradable products is on the rise. Similarly, the biological nutrients can replace non-renewable and toxic inputs and safely degrade in the natural environment after use. Some organizations are deploying technical nutrients, which are inputs like metals and minerals that are capable of being reused and recycled infinitely if they are not contaminated or leaked in the value chain.

A company like Nike is driving circularity at scale through the implementation of a design and manufacturing process that reuses and recycles footwear manufacturing scrap and post-consumer shoe waste, converting it into Nike Grind material. This material is recycled into athletic surfaces such as courts and tracks through a partnership with companies like Astroturf. 71% of Nike shoes are made from waste materials. Similarly, Johnson Controls uses a circular supply chain and reverse logistics network to design, make, transport, recycle and recover vehicle batteries. It has reached a 99% recycling rate for conventional batteries in North America, Europe, and Brazil, whilst their sold batteries are now made up of 80% recycled materials.

The concept of sharing platform is gaining momentum as it fights with low utilization of assets. Airbnb, which operates as an online marketplace for people to lease or rent short-term lodging, participate or facilitate tourist experiences or make restaurant reservations, provides a wonderful example of platform sharing. The company has more than 4 million listed lodgings in 65,000 cities and an annual turnover of $2.6bn.

Over the last few years, there has been a shift in consumer behavior towards the "access-over-ownership" mindset. This model requires the manufacturers and retailers to bear the total cost of product ownership, offering it to customers as a service. The customers become more of users rather than product owners. This model facilitates a shift towards longevity, reliability, and reusability as performance and durability take precedence over disposability. Isn't it a win-win situation for the companies and customers?

The companies gain a new revenue stream while customers realize significant cost savings, superior performance, quality, and reduced risk of ownership. For example, Michelin Solutions has adopted product as a service model by offering tire as a service. The company leases sensor-enabled tires to fleet customers, effectively selling a service that is monetized per kilometers driven. Customers don't own the tires and therefore don't have the responsibility of maintenance. Extending the lifecycle of tires would save consumption of more than 400 million tires and save 35 million tons of emissions globally.

In the end, the idea of implementing a circular economy may just be one way to make us aware that we need a more encompassing, integrated, and restorative sustainability path that needs more and more people and businesses to participate. We cannot run ahead with technology without keeping a watch on the waste we are generating or without considering the burden on our Mother Earth.

"When you talk about saving the planet, you turn it into an ethical question, and I think you won't solve problems if they are ethical."
— Michael Braungart

Arresting climate change is not a subject for the weak-hearted. It needs us to rationalize our resources and strength across every fabric of our life. Neither can the government leave the topic, nor can we. Various business houses have come forward as a part of their corporate social responsibility; however, in this melee, we can never underestimate the contribution of the common man.

The industries are indeed the biggest clog as they arm-twist the government for their own benefits. However, consumers cannot be brainwashed so easily. If we, the consumers, understand the game plan of the linear economy, we can force everyone to change for the betterment of the world. Next time you buy something, realize that you have got the item or service you wanted as a buyer. However, the same item has brought in something you didn't ask for.

It may be harmful to you and your loved ones. Once you understand the destruction that is taking place on the very bosom of Mother Earth, you must come forward and do something to change it. Even if you never intended to cause such destruction, you have unintentionally and unknowingly become a part of this strategy of tragedy. Either you can continue to be engaged in that strategy of tragedy, or you can design and implement a strategy of change. And believe me, the latter is only the way out.

Only circular economy and the closed-loop system of the supply chain can build our path to revive Mother Earth. Once you learn the nitty-gritty of a circular economy, you understand how everyone, big or small, rich or poor, has a role to play.

Instead of remaining the spectator of climate change, buckle up and implement a new mindset to change.

5

WASTE NOT
Think Ahead – Think Different

It was September 23, 2019. The whole of humanity was dumbfounded as Greta Thunberg, a teenage Swedish girl, stood on the podium and took the UN Climate Action Summit by storm. Her outcry pierced through the dreaded path of Earth's deteriorating condition as she demanded a logical answer from all those imperious world leaders. Her words were loud and forceful as she conveyed the threats, concerns, and fears she faced about her life and future in a world that has been made unfit for human living.

Do not scowl at her 'How Dare You'. It was not mere teenage angst fueled by an adrenaline rush. There is a saying in the world of Google, that within five random searches one would land on a page talking about Adolf Hitler. But, do you know that five random searches on science are likely to land you on a page that denounces science and technology as the biggest curse of human existence? Every second weblink opens up to an appalling picture of plastic waste littered and dumped in the water canals.

Or can we forget the photo of a huge turtle trapped and choking inside a polythene bag going viral over the internet? Oceans have been the largest dustbin for human waste: biodegradable or otherwise. Ask students to write an essay on science and technology and they all will jostle to find the flaws in the system. The whole world curses the invention of plastic, all the while blissfully ignoring the magnificent science behind its invention.

Today, when you are ready to throw out your garbage, take a minute to analyze if everything in your dustbin is a waste with no value at all. Believe me, at least one-fourth of your daily waste is recyclable or reusable. The mobile case you have dumped into your bin, the old bucket you threw out the other day, those single-use plates you used for that get-together are some of the creations of chemistry that have indeed made your life easy. The prevailing problem does not actually lie in the creation of plastic; rather it is the overuse and improper dumping of plastic waste that has created chaos.

"We don't need a handful of people doing zero waste perfectly. We need millions of people doing it imperfectly."
– Anne Marie Bonneau

There is no such thing called 'away.' The waste you generate on a daily basis may go away from you, but it is going somewhere, getting dumped somewhere. Science is a boon. As humans moved from the protection of caves, science came to their rescue as they made a niche for themselves, the most wonderful creations of God. Unfortunately, unbridled greed to control nature and unabashed anthropocentrism have placed humans in this pitiable state of living. We, humans, are hardcore producers. We have thrived to invent new things, drafted a new dimension toward our comfort while ignoring the repercussions. Let me tell you here, the man who invented plastic did not actually realize that humans would be thoughtlessly dumping tons of non-biodegradable plastic on the Earth or into the oceans.

The science of nuclear chemistry was unveiled to let humanity think of a massive energy source. Those atoms never asked anyone to build atom bombs or nuclear weapons. The incredible creation of science and technology is always a boon to the world of humans until humans realize the limitations before over-consumption.

Today, before dumping your plastic waste, think once if it is avoidable or the waste is recyclable. The world needs us to see things through a fresh lens. The scorching state of pollution has been created by the waste we generate. We are indeed the creators of this problem and if we wish to be part of the solution, we must abandon our imbecile thinking. The path ahead is going to be exhausting; however, as we wish to think ahead, we must think differently.

A Sneak Peek

Necessity has always been the mother of invention. Every invention in science has been a product of human curiosity and a prevailing problem. As the present generation finds plastic to be the equivalent of Frankenstein's monster, let me take you on the journey of its creation. The first synthetic polymer was invented in 1869 by John Wesley Hyatt. That year, a New York firm had offered a reward of $10,000 for anyone who could provide a substitute for ivory. The growing popularity of billiards had put a strain on the supply of natural ivory. After all, slaughtering of wild elephants was becoming a burden, to say the least. Hyatt derived cellulose from cotton fiber and treated it with camphor and discovered a new product that could be crafted into a variety of shapes. Incidentally, the chemical produced could be made to imitate natural substances like tortoiseshell, horn, linen, and ivory.

It brought in a new revolution, as for the first time, human manufacturing was not constrained by the limits of nature. This development helped not only people but also the environment. Advertisements praised celluloid as the savior of the elephant and the tortoise. Plastics could protect the natural world from the destructive forces of human need.

Moreover, the creation of new materials also helped free people from the social and economic constraints imposed by the scarcity of natural resources. Inexpensive celluloid made material wealth more widespread and obtainable. And the plastics revolution was only getting started.

Another big change came in when Leo Baekeland invented Bakelite in 1907. It was the first fully synthetic plastic without using any natural resources. Baekeland had been searching for a synthetic substitute for shellac, a natural electrical insulator, to meet the needs of the rapidly electrifying United States. Bakelite was not only a good insulator, but it was also durable, heat resistant, and unlike celluloid, could fit into mechanical mass production. Bakelite could be shaped or molded into almost anything, providing endless possibilities. It was a huge revolution, not only in the world of polymer science but also instilled new hope in the industries. The product was soon marketed as the material of a thousand uses. Soon, Hyatt's and Baekeland's successes led major chemical companies to invest in the research and development of new polymers, and new plastics soon joined celluloid and Bakelite. While Hyatt and Baekeland had been searching for materials with specific properties, the new research programs sought new plastics for their own sake and worried about finding uses for them later. The pursuit of plastic continued and soon the marvel of chemistry led humans to a plethora of options where plastics become a household name.

World War II necessitated a great expansion of the plastics industry in Western countries. The need to preserve scarce natural resources made the production of synthetic alternatives a priority. Plastics provided those substitutes. Nylon was invented by Wallace Carothers in 1935 as synthetic silk, which was used during the war for parachutes, ropes, body armor, helmet liners, and more. Plexiglas provided an alternative to glass for aircraft windows. As years passed by, plastics have been turned to new uses for their adaptability. As the famous author Susan Freinkel said, *"In product after product, market after market, plastics challenged traditional materials and won, taking the place of steel in cars, paper and glass in packaging, and wood in furniture."*

Today, if we are overcrowded with plastic products, it is because the possibilities of plastics gave humanity a utopian vision of a future with abundant material wealth. Plastic is an inexpensive, safe sanitary substance that could be shaped by humans according to their whims.

This immaculate optimism about plastics did not last very long though. The perception toward plastics no longer remained unambiguously positive as the plastic debris took refuge in the oceans. Gradually, the intellectuals started talking over the environmental problems. Rachel Carson's 1962 book, Silent Spring, exposed the dangers of chemical pesticides. Then again, a major oil spill occurred off the California coast, and the Cuyahoga River in Ohio, dumped with plastic waste, caught fire. Such incidents kept happening now and then and soon more and more people spread awareness about environmental issues. If anyone ever looks out for a metaphor for persistence, plastic is the best. The weight of plastic waste kept growing over the decades and soon humans started thinking of turning away from plastic. However, is it feasible?

Complete abandonment of plastic is not a way out. Think of the women who have to cross miles after miles to carry water. Isn't the plastic vessel a respite for them? Can you lift a metal bucket filled with water?

However, plastic became a special target because plastic is considered 'immortal' in the sense that it lasts forever in the environment. Considering the wide spectrum of plastic utility, recycling can be a better solution. Despite growing mistrust, plastics are critical to modern life. Plastics made possible the development of computers, cell phones, and most of the lifesaving advances of modern medicine. Lightweight and good for insulation, plastics help save fossil fuels used in heating and transportation.

Perhaps most important, inexpensive plastics raised the standard of living and made material abundance more readily available. Without plastics, many of the possessions that we take for granted might be out of reach for most. Replacing natural materials with plastic has made many of our possessions cheaper, lighter, safer, and stronger. And we cannot deny that.

The fact is plastics have taken a valuable place in our lives. And right now, our attempt to combat the climate crisis should focus on managing the waste. We cannot go back to the past and undo the invention. All we can do is to strategically use plastic and recycle it in every possible way to increase its longevity.

In short, the idea is to make plastic use and reuse more sustainable. There is a multitude of innovations going on and the scientific community has come up with the concept of bioplastics. Apparently, it reduces the use of fossil fuels for producing plastic and invariably ends with biodegradation. Isn't that amazing? Some innovators are searching for ways to make recycling more efficient, and they even hope to perfect a process that converts plastics back into the fossil fuels from which they were derived. Honestly, humans have realized the impending grimness and are working toward combating it. Plastics are not perfect; nevertheless, they are an important and necessary part of our future.

The story of the climate crisis cannot be painted only with the stain of plastics now, can it? Over the centuries, every slice of science and technology has changed our lives and behaviors in society. Today, the present world is ruminating over the problem of excess and unwarranted appetite of human needs. But then, who constructed this need for everything? Many decades ago, an Indian who had crossed oceans to live his American dream could never think of chatting with his family through WhatsApp. But the present generation, 'millennial kids,' can enjoy that emotional relief, thanks to technology.

From holding a pen to writing the history of humanity on the surface of the moon, science and technology have been more than a blessing to the human race. We all simply use technology to survive, evolve, and attain progress by creating a greater level of efficiency. Could you think of Zoom meetings in the last century? Before this Covid pandemic, the world faced the pandemic of the Spanish Flu in 1918. People were locked down and battled death without the hope of medicines or vaccines. We cannot blame the intelligent minds who tried to show us a better path.

It is utterly inappropriate to frown at the world of science and technology because it is the same science that can lead us to the escape route. Evolving technology has kept providing us with amazing resources that can bring a vast difference to our everyday lives.

As human society continues to thrive in the modern world, our outlook should be focused on finding a solution rather than griping over the problem. Precautions and preservation are the two weapons we have now. The infiltration of technology and novel products into our lives has been gradual without us realizing the extent to which technology has become a part of our every waking moment. From the tiny to the enormous, every application of modern technology is opening a new world to us. And here, instead of panicking or complaining over scientific inventions or plastic waste, we ought to mold our thinking like plastic—Pliant to Change.

A Curse So Overwhelming

"Only we humans make waste that nature can't digest."
– Charles Moore

Amidst the pandemonium of pollution, the biggest curse on humanity is the overwhelming burden of plastic. Pliable, moldable, and malleable, plastic is one of the wonders created by humans, but plastic waste has been a problem for two decades now. Some plastics cannot be recycled, and of course, once dumped into the landfills, they do not rot. If there is going to be another apocalypse and the Earth ever rejuvenates, it will not be surprising to find plastics as fossils. The point is, plastic has no scavenger on Earth. It lingers and litters every stratum of the ecosystem. Let us have a quick look at the detrimental effects of our excessive use of plastic objects.

Plastics do not decompose in nature on their own. So, the polythene bags thrown away carelessly on roads and other places get into drains and sewers. These plastic bags block the drains and sewers, often causing dirty drain water to spill on the roads.

During heavy rains, the choked drains and sewers are not able to carry away all the rainwater quickly and hence a flood-like situation is created in the city areas. Many of us fill household garbage in plastic bags and throw it away. When stray cattle look for food in this thrown garbage, they also eat up the plastic bags along with the waste food. The cattle cannot distinguish between food and plastic and the latter balloons up inside the stomach of the animal and causes its untimely and painful death. Sometimes plastic bags that have been used earlier for storing poisonous substances are thrown into garbage dumps; these are picked by rag pickers, washed, and resold to shopkeepers in the market. The use of such plastic bags for packing and storing cooked food materials can harm our health. For carrying and storing food products, we should use only new plastic bags or containers that are approved for such use. The burning of plastic waste materials gives out extremely harmful gases that not only cause air pollution but are also carcinogenic to humans.

Now, we all are aware of the problem; so, what can we do to minimize our contribution toward plastic waste? We should reuse plastic carry bags for shopping purposes, which will minimize the number of plastic bags used by us. You can understand the grim situation as most of the shops and shopping malls charge you these days when you ask for polythene bags. Can we not go back to our olden days and use cloth bags? In fact, many renowned clothing brands and grocery chains have started delivering their products in paper bags. Start reusing the plastic vessels. A ghee bottle, once used can be washed thoroughly and reused to store salt, spices, or pickles. Your kitchen should be sustainable by generating less waste. Having a glossy, showy kitchen such as seen in modular kitchen adverts is not important.

Remember, style is not what can save the Earth, but rather sustainability. Get in touch with recycling industries or outlets to let your unavoidable plastic waste enjoy the benefits of the circular economy. The more garbage we generate in our day-to-day life, the more difficult it will be to get rid of. One of the concrete ways to overcome this problem is to reduce waste generation.

How can we do that?

- We should dispose of our kitchen garbage by vermicomposting to obtain high-quality manure for our plants. We should never put kitchen garbage in polythene bags and throw it away.
- We should not throw out plastic bags carelessly after use. The plastic bags and other plastic containers should be reused wherever possible.
- We should make full use of the pages in our notebooks, etc., by writing on both sides. Can we not go back to our childhood days of using the slate, at least where it is feasible to do so? Learning will become more economical and also environment friendly.
- Are you sending used newspapers, magazines, and notebooks for recycling?
- Donate. There can be no better job than that in a world where one person's waste is another's basic need. We should give old clothes and books to others who can use them.
- We should use cloth handkerchiefs instead of paper tissues to save paper and reduce the generation of garbage.
- Change your purchasing perspective. We should choose and buy products with the least packaging.
- We should recycle the old and useless objects made of glass and metals instead of   throwing them away.
- Follow all the steps of the waste hierarchy. Reduce. Reuse. Recycle.

Do understand that waste disposal is not the responsibility of only the Government; it is also the responsibility of each one of us. All of us should take steps to reduce the generation of garbage as much as possible. The NIMBY perspective should change for the betterment of humans and Mother Earth.

Discarding of waste, global pollution, and the associated climate change must be tackled soon and strategically. After all, it is not only the humans who are in danger but the whole ecosystem.

"It is the worst times, but it is the best of times because we still have a chance."
– Sylvia Earle

And before you conclude that the WASTE NOT concept is not feasible, let me remind you of Lauren Singer. She is considered the queen of the zero-waste world who has been living a zero-waste lifestyle since 2012 and dedicates her time to increasing awareness about the plastic waste problem and helping to make a difference. In her words, trash is for the tossers and there is no better life than the zero-waste life.

Whopping Waste – Niggling Management

We look at our littered streets, cover our nostrils tight as we cross a dump yard, and of course curse the wicked state of affairs. This behavior is omnipresent. We overlook our own flaws, but are quite intent on keeping tabs on where the others are going wrong. Are you aware that an average American produces almost eight times more municipal solid waste than what the average Indian produces? Consider the use of kitchen tissues, packaged food, and the archetypical western lifestyle: they are bound to be the maximum waste generators. Similarly, an average European produces far more e-waste than the average Indian does. Can you believe that an average Indian uses fewer plastic materials than that used by the average Westerner? Even then, the Western countries look so picture perfect and the ultimate portrayal of cleanliness.

Why?

Because, although our waste is whopping, the waste management is niggling—ineffective and improper to the core.

Let me tell you that our municipal solid waste can be classified into five main categories:

- Recyclable material – Glass, bottles, cans, paper, metals, certain plastic, etc.
- Composite wastes – Tetra packs and waste plastics such as toys, waste clothing.
- Biodegradable wastes – Paper, food and kitchen waste, green waste, basically anything that is a product of nature.
- Inert waste – Dirt, rocks, construction and demolition waste, debris.
- Domestic hazardous waste and toxic waste – E-waste, medication, light bulbs, fluorescent tubes, shoe polish, chemicals, paints, batteries, fertilizers and pesticide containers, spray cans, etc.

Do you know that even a half-literate European knows how to segregate the waste? The decisive factor here is the common man's knowledge about waste segregation at the source. Waste management is not an innate mechanism for humans. We have to teach our brains to do it. And in this pursuit, governing bodies, the government, and various social organizations must take this initiative to bring in behavioral change. Western countries often face a huge accumulation of waste in public places during the weekends. The dark alleys behind pubs, football stadiums, and streets are more often found heavily littered. So, how do they manage this condition? In the early hours of Monday morning, the streets are machine cleaned and vacuumed, and by the time people wake up to the new week ready for work, they look perfect.

Can it not be implemented on the Indian roads? Probably yes; the machines can be customized to our roads. However, it is a paradigm shift for the administration. Are we prepared for it? Well, we HAVE to be prepared!

Instead of copying the consumption traits of the Western countries, we must learn from their waste management tactics. As per the records, urban India generates 62 million tons of waste (MSW) annually, and it has been predicted that this will reach 165 million tons by 2030. Annually, 43 million tons of municipal solid waste is collected, out of which 31 million is dumped in landfill sites and just 11.9 million is treated. We cannot deny the recklessness of the administration when we do not find enough public bins. Moreover, how many public bins on the streets are covered? Waste often overflows out of those bins and ends up all over the streets.

Waste transporting vehicles are not even covered in most of the cities and they turn out to be another hand in littering the roads. Now, is it all about administrative issues? Oh! There are Mercedes car owners who surreptitiously drop their garbage bags on the road and speed away! Remember that Anushka Sharma fiasco? The Bollywood actress caught a young man red-handed while dropping a chocolate wrapper on the road. Visit any temple in India and you will be pained to see the amount of litter outside each temple. Earlier, India's roads were mainly littered with banana peels or leaves or foods that are biodegradable. However, the present situation is alarming as the maximum proportion of litter consists of plastic.

The core idea behind managing waste is to segregate the waste at the source. The segregated waste must be properly stored, collected, transported, and treated. On the same note, we have to acknowledge that storing biodegradable waste in a non-biodegradable plastic bag does not solve the problem. In an effective solid waste management model, there should be a goal to reduce, reuse, recover, and recycle waste by using the appropriate technologies. The waste that must be disposed of in landfills should be minimized, and additionally, the landfills should be properly managed so that they do not become a source of greenhouse gases and toxins. But in many cities of India, the waste that is generated is just recklessly dumped in most cases. Some of it is dumped on the streets and some in landfills that are not properly managed, and this ends up polluting the air, soil, and even underground water.

India has an informal recycling sector that consists of waste pickers. They indeed play a crucial role in segregating and recycling waste, but in most cases, they are not formally trained. Whatever suits them, they pick and the rest they burn at landfills to keep themselves warm at night. Setting landfills on fire causes air pollution. Consecutively, as these people are mostly illiterate and have inadequate gear, they are exposed to diseases and injuries. Do you know that the size of the landfills in India is constantly increasing and that it is fast becoming a major concern?

One of the main points to ponder on is India's nature of waste. Contrary to the composition of waste in Western countries, the majority of India's waste is organic, which means that there lies a tremendous opportunity to compost a lot of it. All we have to do is make it possible by practicing the principle of segregation of waste at its source.

When we talk about the segregation of waste at the source, nobody is excused. The waste management crisis is present in every fabric of society. Even the commercial institutions and resident welfare associations are required to partner with the urban local body and segregate waste in different categories as biodegradable, non-biodegradable, construction-demolition, domestic-hazardous, horticulture, sanitary, etc.

Similarly, there should be an emphasis on processing biodegradable waste through on-site composting while the recyclable waste should be given to authorized recyclers or waste pickers. If the Solid Waste Management Rule is properly implemented and is also adopted by the people, believe me, it will transform the waste management system and take it to a conducive level. The problem is universal, the solution too shall come from every corner.

The amount of high-calorific waste is increasing and thus, we must adopt waste segregation at source. Apart from this, there exists waste-to-energy technologies that can process unsegregated and 'high moisture-low calorie' waste too. Humans are inherently shaken by change. It is impossible to change human behavior overnight.

However, it is conclusive that the conundrum is about waste management and not only about waste. It is high time that all the stakeholders, urban local bodies, non-governmental organizations, Resident Welfare Associations, Public and Private institutions, and Waste Management Startups, get interlinked and benefit from a combination of centralized and decentralized waste management systems. The key to successful waste management is a decentralized system of composting biodegradable waste. On the sidelines, informal recycling by waste pickers can be made more organized by training and educating them.

It will be an attempt to reduce the burden on the centralized waste management system, which can be employed in dealing with the waste that demands a large-scale treatment. The centralized system should be focused more on maximum resource extraction from waste and safe disposal of residual waste through waste-to-energy projects. Landfills must be ensured proper management through environmental professionals and qualified engineers. The subdued economy must dedicate time, funds, and other resources for waste management colleges and universities, which can easily cater to the rising demand for skilled professionals.

From an Indian perspective, a proper waste management system impacts positively on public healthcare. Additionally, those frequently occurring city floods can be avoided, new jobs will be created, and people will start looking at waste as an opportunity to create wealth.

Eventually, humanity's mission to save Mother Earth can create financial benefits too. Our country is a growing economy, and as its citizens, we should ensure that we avoid reaching the dangerous levels of the average Westerner in plastic consumption and waste production. Much like how prevention is better than cure, waste reduction is better than any kind of waste management. And as Indians, we can always encompass our traditional wisdom of *Aparigraha*. Is there any better approach than that? In essence, the way out has always been at the back of our mind; however, we have failed to recall it.

Embrace the Waste Hierarchy

The threat of poor waste management is well-pronounced in low-income countries where the waste-collection rate itself is poor. Piles of garbage along river banks; thick smoke from open burning of mixed, and partly toxic, waste; pungent odors; flies and rodents— are they not familiar scenes around us? Ever-faster population growth, urbanization, and economic development are producing increasing quantities of waste that are overburdening existing waste-management systems. Public waste systems in cities are unable to keep pace with urban expansion.

In the last few decades, rapid industrialization has happened in countries that have not yet developed the appropriate systems to deal with hazardous and special wastes. In short, the growing trade in waste poses significant challenges and waste management has become one of the most complex and cost-intensive public services. We have to acknowledge that a large chunk of municipal budgets goes into organizing and supporting an effective waste management system. Once we decide to play our role in the game, we have to understand the basic concept of the waste hierarchy.

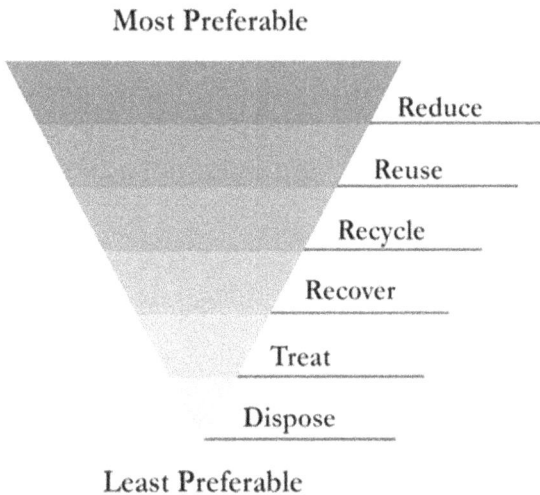

Most Preferable

Reduce

Reuse

Recycle

Recover

Treat

Dispose

Least Preferable

The waste hierarchy embraces three key levels.

- Avoidance: An attempt to reduce the amount of waste generated by households, industry, and all levels of government.

- Resource Recovery: It is vocal about reuse, recycling, reprocessing, and energy recovery, consistent with the most efficient use of the recovered resources.

- Disposal: This is to manage all disposal options in the most environmentally responsible manner.

Let me shut all those curious questions.

Why should I avoid or reduce waste?

Avoiding and reducing the generation of waste encourages the community, industry, and government to reduce the amount of virgin materials extracted and used. Our goal should be to maximize efficiency and avoid unnecessary consumption.

How can there be any resource in waste?

Go to YouTube and search for a recycling video. You can make a jeans handbag from a torn pair of jeans. Everything we waste can have a second chance in some other form. Resource recovery maximizes options for reuse, recycling, reprocessing, and energy recovery.

Sometimes it is impossible to avoid or recover!

Indeed. When avoiding and reducing waste is not possible, the next most preferred option is to reuse the materials without further processing, avoiding the costs of energy and other resources required for recycling. For example, many household and industrial items can be repaired, reused, sold, or donated to charities. Next time when you think of throwing your old mixer-grinder, rethink.

Reuse (without further processing) and recycling (processing waste materials to make the same or different products) keep materials in the productive economy and benefit the environment by decreasing the need for new materials and waste absorption. But then, if further recycling is not feasible, it may be possible to recover the energy from the material and feed that back into the economy where this is acceptable to the community. Apart from this, some materials may be inappropriate to reuse, recycle, or recover for energy and instead require treatment to stabilize them and minimize their environmental or health impacts.

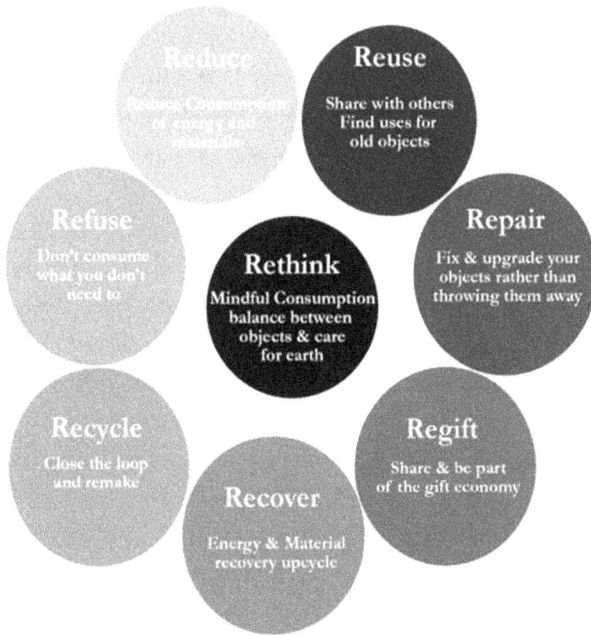

Why disposal is least preferred?

The waste hierarchy recognizes that some types of waste, such as hazardous chemicals or asbestos, cannot be safely recycled and direct treatment or disposal is the most appropriate management option.

However, we should be vigilant in identifying the type of waste before disposing it. Improper waste management practices have jeopardized basic human needs such as clean water, clean air, and safe food.

Moreover, it has brought in severe consequences for public health. Poor waste collection can lead to the spread of disease and improper waste disposal: for example, hazardous waste mixed with household waste can be extremely harmful to workers in the waste sector, adjacent communities, and the environment.

Besides having serious economic, environmental, and health implications, unsound waste management has a social dimension. Like most environmental hazards, deficiencies in waste management disproportionately affect poorer communities as waste is often dumped on land adjacent to slums. Left with the choice between going hungry and waste picking, one percent of the urban population in developing countries choose to sort through the litter on dumps and dirty streets.

Even in countries with proper waste management systems, simply collecting and disposing of the waste out of sight is not a solution. Waste management is not about 'throwing away.' Realize that today's 'away' is going to be your child's backyard tomorrow or, worse, might have already impaired the health of the next generation.

A lot of the waste that we discard can be prevented by changing the design of a product, producing more with fewer resources, reusing, recycling, etc. However, there will always be some waste that cannot be prevented and will require proper handling. Either way, maintaining the homeostasis of our surroundings is critical and can be achieved through understanding the different levels of the waste hierarchy.

"I wrapped my Christmas presents early this year, but I used the wrong paper. See, the paper I used said 'Happy Birthday' on it. I didn't want to waste it so I just wrote 'Jesus' on it."
— Demetri Martin

The way we look at things matters. The way we conceive our world matters. Change is inevitable: sometimes forced and at times out of sheer necessity. Right now, humanity is trading with the latter. Embrace the change. Embrace the old perspective of reduce-reuse-repair to build a new world.

What Can We Do To Reduce Waste?

It takes a willing attitude to change and contribute toward the betterment of our environment. Whether you are at home or office or school, you have a way out to reduce the amount of waste you generate daily.

Tips for the Home

- The best place to start making a difference is right in your own courtyard. Let us plan our way to reduce, reuse, and recycle materials to decrease household waste.
- Learn to compost at home. Use food scraps, yard trimmings, and other organic wastes to create a compost pile. Adding the compost to the soil increases water retention, decreases erosion, and keeps organic materials out of landfills.
- Raise the cutting height of your lawnmower during the hot summer months to keep the grass roots shaded and cooler. That will help in reducing weed growth, browning, and the need for watering.
- If you need large lawn and garden equipment, such as tillers and chainsaws, you can reduce waste (and save money) by setting up a sharing program with your neighbors.
- When you mow, leave the grass clippings for they return nutrients to the soil. Do not send them for deposition in the landfills.
- If your culture follows the principle of 'return gifts' on auspicious occasions, gift plants to people.

- Use insulation made from recycled paper, glass, and other recovered materials.
- Turn off or unplug lights during the day. Doing so will save energy and help your lights last longer.
- Storms can cause power outages. Prevent waste by keeping rechargeable batteries for your flashlights. If you do use disposable batteries, reduce hazardous waste by buying ones with low mercury content.
- Have a yard sale to find homes for clothes, toys, appliances, and books that you no longer need.
- While shifting, use old newspapers to wrap fragile materials.
- Choose moving boxes with the highest content of recycled paper and bubble wrap containing recycled plastic. Be sure to recycle the packaging materials after your move.
- Be sure to properly dispose of any non-recyclable items that you will not be taking with you.
- For cleaning chores, buy reusable mops, rags, and sponges. When using cleaning products, use only the amount you need and follow the instructions on the container for use and disposal.

Tips for School Premises

Our schools are a shrine of learning and the maker of our behaviors. There are many changes we must implement in our next generation right from their childhood.

- Think green before you shop. Before starting the new school year, look through last year's materials. Many items can be reused or recycled.
- Purchase and use school supplies made from recycled products, such as pencils made from old blue jeans and binders made from old shipping boxes.
- Keep waste out of landfills by using school supplies wrapped in minimal packaging, and buy in bulk.

- Save packaging, colored paper, egg cartons, and other items for arts and crafts projects. And also look for other ways that you can reduce the amount of packing that you throw away.
- If you bring your lunch to school, package it in reusable containers instead of disposable ones. Carry food in reusable plastic or cloth bags, and bring drinks in a thermos instead of in disposable bottles or cartons.
- When buying lunch, grab only what you need. Too often extra ketchup packets and napkins go to waste.
- Remember to recycle your cans and bottles after you finish eating.
- Teachers can set up a composting program at school.
- Be the voice for change. Seeing a child doing the right thing motivates older people.

How to reduce waste at work?

- Engage and motivate your coworkers to buy green products and help reduce waste.
- Instead of printing hard copies of your documents, save them to your hard drive or email them to yourself to save paper.
- Make your printer environment friendly. Change your printer settings to make double-sided pages. Use small point fonts and the "fast draft" setting wherever possible to save ink.
- Pay your bills via e-billing programs, when possible, to save paper.
- Use paperclips (over staples) when possible. Reuse envelopes with metal clasps and reuse file folders by sticking a new label over the previous one.
- Purchase recycled paper and keep a recycling bin near your desk.

- Plan your festive days well
- Festive days are the best time to connect with family and friends, but parties and gift-giving often create extra waste.
- Think green before you shop at the festive sales. Bring your own reusable cloth bag for carrying your purchases, and try to buy items with minimal packaging and/or that are made with recycled content.
- Wrap gifts in recycled or reused wrapping paper. Also remember to save or recycle your used wrapping paper.
- Store all those festive snacks in reusable containers.
- When gifting flowers, consider buying long-lasting silk flowers, potted plants, or live bushes, shrubs, or trees that can be planted in the spring as gifts.
- If you host a party, set the table with cloth napkins and reusable dishes, glasses, and silverware.
- Be sure your guests know where to properly dispose of and recycle their wastes at your party. After holiday festivities, put leftovers in recyclable containers, and share them with family, friends, or others. Donate untouched leftovers from parties to a local food bank or a homeless shelter.

Even while traveling you can do your bit.

Travelers create a lot of waste, even with the best intentions. Whether you are traveling for business or pleasure, you can do a few simple things that will reduce your waste, conserve resources, and minimize the overall environmental impact of your visit.

- When visiting beaches and parks, be sure to take back everything you bring in, so that you can leave places without littering them.
- Hot summer days make you thirsty. Be sure to recycle your used drink containers.

- Consider putting a filter on your water tap and refilling bottles with the filtered water. Instead of buying many small drink bottles, buy drink mixes in bulk and fill your reusable bottles.
- Share the ride and the road. Public transportation and carpooling reduce pollution.
- Take used or damaged car batteries to auto stores that stock or repair lead-acid batteries for safe disposal. The batteries contain toxic amounts of lead and acid, and should not be thrown out with your regular trash.
- Return used car tires to retailers or wholesalers that recycle or retread them. Tires are banned from most landfills, and illegally dumped tires become breeding grounds for mosquitoes and other pests.
- Make sure your car has a clean air filter—a dirty air filter can increase your car's fuel consumption by as much as 10 percent.
- Instead of sending your low-value car to a landfill, offer it to a local charity.
- Have you thought of e-cycling?
- Donate your old computers and tablets to a school. Many schools will be able to make good use of your old machine.
- Before replacing a computer that no longer fits your needs, consider enhancing the computer's capacity by upgrading the hard drive or memory. It saves money.
- Donating used (but still operating) electronics for reuse extends the lives of valuable products and keeps them out of the waste stream for a longer period.
- Be smart with your smartphone! It contains precious raw materials.

S. POCHENDER

"Solid Wastes are the discarded leftovers of our advanced consumer society. This growing mountain of garbage and trash represents not only an attitude of indifference toward valuable natural resources, but also a serious economic and public health problem."

– Jimmy Carter

Handling Plastic Waste in Agriculture

We cannot deny that plastic has literally encroached into every sphere of our economy. The agricultural sector, which forms the backbone of a country, is one of the largest commercial consumers of plastic for sheeting, twining, and packaging. As the food crisis is approaching at a fast rate, every corner of our world is turning vocal toward increasing the local produce. The use of Polytunnels has gained much momentum, though many calls it scarring the agricultural landscape.

As stated earlier, we cannot completely withdraw ourselves from the benefits of plastic. However, as the love for plastic is eternalized amongst the farmers, we must stop these agricultural plastic wastes from going to landfills. We must be loud and clear about abandoning the practice of single use. As per the UN Food and Agriculture Organization, around 12.5 million tons of plastic are used in agriculture every year.

The usage varies from crops and livestock to aquaculture and forestry. The plastic used in the scope of agricultural practices is only 3.5 percent of the total plastic produced globally. And considering the longevity and other benefits of plastic, the production of plastic has been increasing. Amidst all the statistics, the vital question is how these non-biodegradable agricultural plastic waste should be handled? The global outlook reflects that agricultural plastic waste is hardly recycled. In the UK, only 30 percent of non-packaging agri-plastics, such as polytunnels and bale wrap, are collected for reuse. Chemical containers for packaging go back to landfills. However, the Food and Agriculture Organization described that the disastrous use of plastics in the farming sector receives less public attention.

132

It is in fact, far less than that received by the consumer equivalent, and less than other sources of harm to the environment. The trouble is, our world is hungry and these agricultural plastics help grow more food.

It is well proven that yields in polytunnels are higher than that of produce grown in the open. The soil retains more moisture and weeds do not grow that easily. This in turn cuts the need for pesticides. Sheets of plastic bale wrap are also often essential for storing feed in winter. Plastics indeed play a crucial role in farm life and have environmental benefits; however, everything works out in favor of the environment if we efficiently collect the plastic on the farm and introduce it to recycling.

In countries like the United Kingdom, the government runs a Green Tractor Scheme, which has broken the model of making and discarding agri-plastics. It collects and processes the plastic and aims to enable farmers to have all their packaging recycled before 2030. Under the UK's Green Tractor Scheme, there runs a farm assurance rule, which demands evidence of legitimate disposal, preferably for recycling and reuse. Isn't it good?

Every consumer of plastic should be educated to learn about the mistakes and the loopholes. Similarly, since 2010, Canada's Cleanfarms has recovered more than 45,700 tons of plastic containers, and 1,400 tons of grain bags, film, and twine from 1,600 collection sites in Canada. Cleanfarms Contractors take this to centralized locations, shred it, and turn it into new plastic.

While some countries have started to ban farm plastics from being burnt, countries like the UK have implemented a plastic packaging tax. Importers or producers will have to pay a tax on products that contain less than 30 percent recycled material. Instead of dumping the agri-plastic waste, we have to understand the benefits of recycled agri-plastics. They can be used on farms as fencing or for the protection of seedlings and drainage tiles.

Other sectors such as construction use it for sheeting or insulation. However, collection and recycling are two different aspects.

Sorting out the recyclable plastic waste from the whole bunch is crucial. For every kilogram that comes out as new and recycled plastic, the collectors have to pick up twice that weight. Farmers of the last century would not have heard or seen this dramatic usage of plastics on the farmland. However, the times have changed, the climate has changed, and amidst this alacrity of cultivating and securing food for the growing population, the agricultural landscape too had to evolve. There is no escape from plastic in any avenue of life. All we have to do is to channel our efforts strategically to save money by proper waste management.

> *"Take care of the waste on the farm and turn it into useful channels should be the slogan of every farmer."*
> – George Washington Carver

Green Infrastructure – Rise Of The New Dawn

Any practice that uses or replicates natural systems to achieve the desired outcome is considered green infrastructure. When urbanization has gained unstoppable momentum, green infrastructure comes to our rescue when we think of saving Mother Earth. What does the green infrastructure do? Green roofs, bio-swales, and rain gardens. Green roofs replicate meadows to retain water and restore habitats on the top of buildings.

We have to understand that green infrastructure is not synonymous with vegetation. For example, permeable surfaces are considered green infrastructure as well, because they handle rainfall the same way natural landscapes do. Green infrastructure emphasizes restoring and replicating ecological systems to create human benefits. It is indeed a radical migration from our dominant approach of grey infrastructure. How do they differ from each other? Let us take the example of stormwater. Grey infrastructure is designed to quickly divert water as it considers water as something to avoid. However, green infrastructure sees water as a resource. It is valuable for keeping landscapes and waterways healthy.

With green infrastructure, we can reframe climate challenges as opportunities. Green infrastructure not only reduces the load on aging gray infrastructure but also provides opportunities to nourish plants and provide drinking water. Is that all? Wait, there is more! The benefits of green infrastructure are numerous and multifaceted. Several challenges of urban life could be easily solved through green infrastructure. When it is hot, we can rely on green infrastructure to reduce the urban heat island. Plants absorb solar energy for photosynthesis and provide cooling through evapotranspiration.

Vegetation can also shade buildings and nearby surfaces, which decreases the demand for cooling. Cooler environments and less energy production result in less amount of smog. Green infrastructure is very effective at lessening the direct and indirect health effects of hot weather. Similarly, when it rains, we can retain and infiltrate water where it falls with green infrastructure. The retained rainfall penetrates the ground and increases the groundwater supply. This reduces runoff, and in turn limits the pollution of waterways and prevents combined sewer overflows.

Combined sewers are essential ingredients of grey infrastructure, which are responsible for collecting both sewage and surface runoff. When the volume of runoff exceeds the sewer's capacity, overflows occur. This contaminates cities with sewage, creating environmental and human health hazards.

Urban green infrastructure provides many social, economic, and environmental benefits. It has the ability to capture and store carbon from the atmosphere through sequestration. Growing urban environments and subsequent increases in greenhouse gas emissions require solutions that assess the potential of our landscapes to act as effective carbon sinks.

With green infrastructure, much can be done to improve upon these human-harnessed ecological systems to maximize their carbon sequestration and limit the emission of biologically-generated green house gases. Green infrastructure improves energy efficiency and reduces cooling loads, driving down emissions created by energy production.

Urbanization has almost snatched the green scenic beauty from the surroundings. Green infrastructure projects that remediate unused urban areas often gift us a dose of nature. These spaces provide habitats for native species as well as relaxation and recreation opportunities for people. Green spaces have been shown to promote community cohesion, decrease stress, and reduce crime. And more than anything, green infrastructure bestows us with an ample dose of nature to revitalize our physical and emotional well-being.

As the famous American social commentator, Will Rogers said, *"Show me a healthy community with a healthy economy and I will show you a community that has its green infrastructure in order and understands the relationship between the built and the unbuilt environment."* We humans have developed a lust for affluence and with each passing year, our behavior toward consumption is becoming psychotic. We are accumulating things we neither need nor enjoy and thus every alternate possession of ours ends in the dump yard. We have been so preoccupied with our possessions that we have almost lost touch with reality. We humans are standing on the threshold of bringing a dramatic change in the way we thrive on Earth. We have to make a clean breast about nature's ability to reform itself.

There is no bigger science or scientist than nature itself. If we sit and disentangle every stage of the waste hierarchy, the answer to our quest for a better world lies in urban green infrastructure. The fact remains the same; we cannot undo what has been done.

Rapid urbanization has led to the inflation of waste generation and greenery has almost vanished from our lives. Besides, there is hardly any respite from the greenhouse gas emissions. Consider Earth as a tent that has been covering you, protecting you from rain, heat, and all kinds of adversities.

You have been happily carrying out all your activities without paying any attention to the condition of the tent. One day, the tent got a hole in one corner. You failed to recognize the problem. As the years passed by, the hole gradually widened and soon you could feel the scorching heat and often got drenched in the rain.

Now, you realize how wrong you have been in overlooking the small hole. However, if you want to survive, you must patch the hole in the tent, no matter how big it has become. This is an accurate depiction of our current situation. We must find out a competitive solution where humans and mother Earth can have a win-win situation.

Along with the plan to reduce our physical waste generation, moving forward to green infrastructure shall help us in combating other factors of the climate crisis too. Proper implementation and maintenance of waste hierarchy and urban green infrastructure is bound to become the major priority for us humans. Implementation of green infrastructure must happen at the individual level too.

If watering plants looks like a daunting job to you, educate yourself about plant varieties that need minimal water for maintenance. Even if you are in an independent house, you can leave some area unpaved and grow plants that will not only beautify your surroundings, but also do the needful for our deteriorating climate. Do not smirk at an individual's role in combatting the climate crisis. You have been a part of the problem and even your smallest contribution is going to add value to this global problem.

Value the statutory necessity of making water pits for the sake of recharging the groundwater. We have to embrace a sustainable lifestyle through a minimalistic approach. Finally, try to hold a different lens as you scrutinize the concept of REDUCE. It is never about having less: it is about making room for everything that truly matters.

Right now, humanity is running a race against the climate crisis. The competitor is unnaturally fast and thus, humans have to devise crucial strategies. Nobody likes to live in a trash can, so it is better if we lend our hands to reducing waste generation by the whole of humanity. Next time you look at your bursting garbage bag, open it and see what all you could have reduced. Waste management is not rocket science; it is about developing compassionate behavior toward Mother Earth.

6

SUSTAINABILITY: THE R's TO SAVE MOTHER EARTH

"We can sit back, do nothing and watch our planet be destroyed. Or we can take action, become advocates and start making lifestyle choices which are kinder to people and the planet."
– Kira Simpson

How would you react if I tell you that minimalizing is actually maximizing? It actually adds profit to your wallet. Sounds ridiculous? As we witness Mother Earth falling prey to our caustic habits, we are in dire need of a sustainable lifestyle. Oh! Change is so difficult.

Let me assure you here that the R's of a sustainable lifestyle is a money-making business. While lending our hand to saving Earth, we all can actually save and make money as well. Now, the route we wish to take depends on us—the minimalistic path to maximize the all-around profit or the exploitive route to further provoke the climate crisis! We all are aware of the Domino effect. The falling row of dominos reflects the cumulative effect produced when one event sets off a chain of similar effects.

Climate change, population growth, and other such extreme events have invariably triggered social crises and instability. We are at the crux of a moment where we must jot down the processes that dominate humanity's emergence, resilience, and collapse. Human activities, the lustful desire to grow, grow, and grow toward affluence have landed us in this ghastly affair of climate change.

Let me tell you that history keeps a record of our ill-treatment and attitude toward Mother Earth. There are unique examples of societies that have failed to develop buffers and strategic resilience against climate change and natural variability. Do we wish to repeat those stories of failed attempts or should we start to plan better? We ARE in the state of PLANETARY EMERGENCY. The world has already crossed the nine tipping points and the effects of global warming can cause a deadly domino effect on all forms of life.

> *"We must unleash world action that accelerates the path towards a world that can continue evolving on a stable planet."*
> – Prof. Johan Rockstrom

Humankind is not the creator of life. This beautiful tapestry of living beings has been woven by nature and Mother Earth. Lives on Earth are blissfully woven into a web where humans are just one thread. All forms of life are bound with each other, whether through a food chain or by sharing an ecosystem. If we cause any harm to the web, we are bound to face dreadful consequences.

It is inescapable. Every ounce of nature is interconnected and any leakage in the balance brings about an avalanche of challenges. The Earth's climate is based on a sensitive balance of many factors. Researchers have found that tipping points and positive feedback destabilize our climate faster than previously thought and the probability of a Domino Effect setting off is very high. A study was conducted by Nicholas Institute of Duke University to showcase the effects of climate change on various aspects of our regular life. Heather Randell, a postdoctoral fellow in the institute presented this flowchart to depict how every aspect of human life is affected.

One problem leads to another and the chain reaction goes on while placing severe implications over our sustenance on Earth.

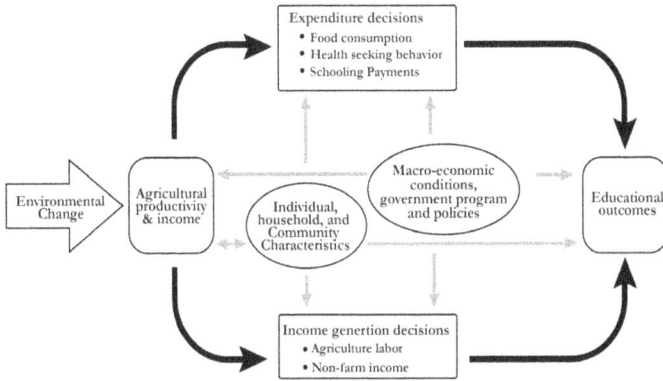

The planet's resources are running out and we need to take steps quickly to adopt habits that are respectful of and healthy for the planet and future generations. Leading a sustainable life means more than just being a responsible consumer. It is a question of living based on a commitment to the environment and making the necessary little changes to our daily lives. According to World Health Organization data, the population on the planet is rising. Each of us has to eat, get about, and consume goods and services. Every human body is more or less equal in its basic needs; however, irresponsible consumerism is creating a huge imbalance in the system.

Improper consumption leads to the immense generation of waste and places an extra burden not only on the Earth's ecosystem but also in our daily life. What if I say there is a way out to keep the problems at bay while making some extra bucks! The concept of 'Sustainable Lifestyle' has come to us as a blessing in disguise. However, does the sustainable lifestyle of a handful of people make a difference? Believe me, every gesture counts.

How? Because each person's reputation serves as a positive reinforcement for others. In other words, the fact that one person bothers to recycle correctly is an inspiration for the others.

According to researchers, encouraging these little actions is as easy as following a few tips and providing environmental education. When we see our leaders holding a broom and cleaning the streets, we are bound to get encouraged. That is how a change can be knitted into our normal life. Next time, when you chuckle and say that it is just one plastic bottle, realize that there are eight billion people behind you who say the same. Just like how every drop of water contributes to the making of an ocean, every bit of waste contributes to the imbalance of the climate.

> *"Each one of us matters, has a role to play, and makes a difference. Each one of us must take responsibility for our own lives, and above all, show respect and love for living things around us, especially each other."*
> – Jane Goodall

Let Us Dig Into The Sustainable Lifestyle

The negative impact of our way of life on the environment has continued to increase. Overexploitation of natural resources, water pollution, soil pollution, and deforestation have irrefutably caused a huge loss of biodiversity. To address these drastic changes and environmental challenges, several social reformers and scientists are getting vocal over sustainable lifestyles. Let us appreciate that any development is sustainable when it meets the needs of the present without compromising the ability of future generations to meet their own needs.

Sustainable living works to reduce personal and societal environmental impact by making positive changes that can, in turn, counteract climate change and other negative environmental concerns. In simple language, sustainable living is a method of reducing one's carbon footprint. It is about empowering people and communities to lead better lives. The present world is stretched thin for resources and under the threat of global biodiversity loss and climate change, our lifestyle decisions are putting the planet at risk. All we need now is targeted actions.

Sustainable living begins by understanding how our lifestyle choices impact the world around us and how we can endeavor for everyone to live better and lighter. None of us wake up intending to harm the environment. Similarly, none of us wake up to help it either. People get up and live their lives and strive toward their aspirations. The number of possessions people have in many parts of the world has shot up, while in other areas, many still struggle to meet their basic needs. Our future now depends on our behavior and how we choose to live, work, and play as global consumers. The way we run our homes, the food we eat, the places we go for relaxation, what we buy, and how we care for our planet—everything contributes toward combating the climate crisis.

Humans do not change their behavior based on what they should do. No matter how much data or statistics about negative future scenarios are provided, they remain preoccupied with their existing lifestyle. We have to understand that we humans just tend to fulfill our needs and aspirations. We make decisions based on price, accessibility, effectiveness, and other additional criteria like well-being or trends.

Sustainability has not been made a defining criterion. Even the ones who want to live in a more sustainable manner often lack information and access to affordable and desirable products and services. This underscores the role of governments and businesses (who are also consumers of resources) in providing more information and supporting positive behavioral change. The authorities must support and develop new business models to make sustainable living a default option.

Sustainable living has become vital for our health and our planet's health. Let us have a quick look at the benefits. Living sustainably can improve our life balance by reducing our dependence on vehicles or machinery. By being less reliant on vehicles, we are more likely to walk or cycle, which helps us create healthier habits.We can also live healthier lives by consuming high-quality, local foods. Consumption of red meats is one the large proponents of climate change.

Moreover, red meats are also unhealthy for our physical health, and by eating less meat-based diets, we can reduce the damage done to our bodies and the planet. We all throw things away, and with almost eight billion people on the planet, isn't that a lot of waste? Landfills are not a healthy option and not a long-term solution, either. Every year, around 150 million tons of trash make it into marine environments. Only compostable products will biodegrade within six months. Of course, our use of fossil fuels to power our homes, businesses, and transportation creates harmful gases that warm our planet and create extreme weather conditions. If we do not act to stop this within the next decade, the damage may be irreversible. Lastly, let me disappoint you a little more. Even biodegradable plastics may outlive us. The only way to curb the dangers hovering around our planet is to incorporate the R's in our lifestyle.

How Many R's Do You Need?

The answer is simple–The More The Merrier. Frankly, the concept of sustainability is not anything new. It all began with the incorporation of 3 basic R's of sustainability: Reduce-Reuse-Recycle. Over the years, when the sustainable lifestyle has become a necessity and requires everyone to participate in building a better world, we realized there is a human factor associated with these R's of the sustainable lifestyle. Let us understand the different R's and see how many R's you have gathered in your sustainable lifestyle.

- **Rethink**

Before you buy something, think if you really need it. Realize that impulse purchases burden our pocket when eventually we end up throwing these out without using them. This is especially common with groceries. Do you know that about one-fourth of food prepared in marriages and other functions go to waste? Imagine the burden on your pocket. Even though you justify this act by donating food to the underprivileged, your donation does not have any effect.

That rich food has so much calorific value that it remains unhealthy for an underprivileged person. Even if you leave aside the food wastage during big functions, you cannot ignore the box of leftovers rotting in your fridge. Reducing food wastage is one of the best ways for us to slow down climate change. So next time be mindful about grabbing veggies if you do not have plans to eat them.

Rethinking is the first change you have to bring while planning for a sustainable lifestyle. How many clothes, makeup products, party decorations, and other stuff get purchased only to be used once or twice and then thrown out. Next time you plan to make a purchase, do ask yourself–

What is its purpose?

How many times will I use it?

Can I recycle it or will it end up in the landfill?

Do I have something at home that I can repurpose into the item?

I am looking to purchase?

Can I repurpose it?

- **Refuse**

Are we not bombarded with free stuff these days? Extra napkins at fast-food restaurants, business cards, pens, and so much more are ours for the taking. More often than not, we take these items home and then throw them straight into our trash bins. Can we not avoid creating that extra waste by not accepting these free items? If you are confident that you will use it, then accept it. Otherwise, politely decline and move on. Initially, it will be awkward sometimes to say no to free stuff but realize the greater goal for saying no. You do not want to bring clutter into your house and you definitely want to keep it out of our landfills.

- **Reduce**

Everyone has heard of the third R of sustainability but do you know how to properly use it? This means reducing the amount of unnecessary stuff you buy and bring into the home. One great way to do this is to invest in sustainable alternatives that will last forever.

Invest in reusable alternatives, which can drastically reduce the waste in your home. More than anything, it is cost-effective. Reducing can also mean to reduce the amount of a product you use to make it last longer. Let me tell you a warped secret of consumerism. Consider a product like a shampoo or a hand wash. The containers are designed such that a single pump or squeeze gives you a huge dollop of the product thus ensuring that it gets empty faster and you buy a new one.

- **Repurpose**

Repurposing is one of the best R's of sustainability. Once something has been used up, instead of throwing it straight into the trash, see if you can repurpose it and use it for something else. This will prevent perfectly good items from going into the landfill. Let me give you some simple examples.

  – Use old moisturizer jars to hold safety pins, coins, or other small items.
  – Glass jars are perfect for holding food or planting new seeds
  – Use old newspapers for arts and crafts
  – Use old toothbrushes to clean tight spaces
  – There are umpteen number of ways to repurpose your possessions. You just have to be creative enough.

- **Reuse**

Extend an item's life by reusing the item until it can no longer function. This is different from repurposing because you are using the item for its original purpose. Whereas when you repurpose, you are using the item for a new purpose. Some examples are the reuse of disposable straws after cleaning them, reuse of clean plastic cutlery in your lunch box, and reusing plastic bags to carry items.

- **Repair**

This is another way to extend the lifetime of items. There are many businesses that will repair items if you fail to do so. It will oftentimes be much cheaper to repair it than to buy a new one. Instead of throwing a torn sandal, go to a cobbler and get it repaired.

- **Recycle**

When it comes to recycling, find out the list of recyclers in your region. Not all regions have recycling facilities that can accept all types of plastic or other wastes.

- **Rot**

The final R of sustainability is rot, i.e., allowing your organic waste like food scraps and grass clippings to decompose through the process of composting. That rotting organic waste can be transformed over time into a nutrient-rich soil enhancer. That same waste in a garbage bag sent to the local landfill will increase greenhouse gas in the form of methane. Even if you use a garbage disposal service, most of the solid waste is simply filtered out at the water treatment facility and rerouted to the landfill. Although a lot of municipalities now have curbside pickup services much like recycling, it is better to start composting in our own backyards.

Change Is The New Trendsetter

People growing up in the last century would know the value of every purchase they make and would hesitate to throw away anything that no longer worked. Earlier this urge to repair and recycle things was termed old-fashioned. However, now, as the climate crisis makes us uneasy, we have renamed it as circular economy for the better.

The older generations used the R's of reduce, reuse, repair, and recycle because they believed in the policy 'waste not, want not,' while now, the R's are coming back in vogue considering the pitiable condition of Mother Earth.Our never-ending resource exploitation has struck a nerve among the environmentalists and we are now bound to follow the circular economy goals for our own sustenance.

A decade ago, the big honchos of the economy took it for granted that consumers would always embrace the most up-to-date versions of digital devices. They would buy upgraded gadgets when their current ones malfunctioned or wore out. This upgrade culture was so ingrained in our consumeristic society that tech companies tended to design products on the assumption that they would quickly become obsolete. They used overt and covert strategies to prompt consumers to keep churning their devices. However, these days, the cost of this upgrade mentality is becoming clear.

Global E-waste Statistics Partnership, which measures electric and electronic waste, estimates that some 53.6 million tons of products were discarded in 2019, that is, 21 percent more than what was discarded five years earlier. Less than 20 percent of this e-waste was officially recorded as recycled. There is a host of initiatives underway to try to change consumer and corporate behaviors. There is always a thrill in buying something new to wear. In recent times, Generation Z is knitting a new outlook. Wearing something new does not mean owning the dress. For many younger shoppers, sharing economy is acceptable and they find ownership to be less important. Moreover, buying jeans second-hand or renting a designer dress has become the new norm.

Even in the big fat Indian weddings, many brides are opting to hire their bridal outfits. Isn't that a major change in the outlook? After all, most of the bridal dresses remain locked in the wardrobe forever! As Georgie Hyatt, co-founder and chief executive of Rotaro, a fashion rental site, stated, *"What we are seeing with young consumers is that 'new' doesn't need to be 'new off the shelf'—it just means new to the consumer."* There is a steep rise in rentals and resale amongst the younger generation. On a similar note, there is a huge partition between the mindset of this younger generation.

According to WGSN, the trend forecaster, the younger breeds are divided into two categories—Gen Me and Gen We. On one side are the trend-focused hyper-consumerists driving the success of fast-fashion giants, such as Shein and Boohoo. On the other, are eco-conscious shoppers who prioritize their sustainable values.

While Gen Me represents the breed of playful aspirants, Gen We belongs to the category of conscious consumers. But either way, the circular economy is able to make some room for itself amidst this Gen Z. The ray of hope is in their acceptance of resale, rentals, and reused products. The tech-savvy younger consumers are resonating well with apps such as Depop, Vestiaire Collective, Poshmark, and Vinted, where users can buy and sell second-hand clothing. Even big retailers such as Asos, H&M, and Levi's have tapped into the resale market. Asos has introduced its own second-hand marketplace in 2010 to allow individuals and small boutiques to sell used clothing.

There is a new wave of change coming. Why? Because along with preserving Mother Earth, the R's of sustainable living help in money saving and money making as well. We are facing a climate crisis, and we CANNOT run behind fashion and trends the way we used to do.

A similar story of upcycling has spurred its head in leftover foods and drinks. Breweries around the world churn out beer to satisfy the world's 200 billion-liters-a-year drinking habit, leaving behind a huge mountain of spent grain, the remains of barley. This spent grain has long been regarded to have low value and sold as cattle feed, or discarded.

But the world's largest brewer, Anheuser-Busch InBev has built a new approach. Extracts from AB InBev's spent grain have been renamed as saved grain and are making their way into food products made by global groups such as Nestlé and Nomad Foods. Two plants, including facilities in St Louis, Missouri, and Belgium costing $200 million, are under construction to process this byproduct into protein and fiber for use as ingredients.

This upcycling of food waste is helping in diminishing the food industry's environmental impact. Food upcycling has become one of the major goals after ambitious climate goals were set out after the 2015 Paris agreement. Food waste makes a significant contribution toward global emissions, around 6 percent to 10 percent, and thus food upcycling is certainly a change to boast about. In 2019, Turner Wyatt, a social entrepreneur from Colorado, US, founded the Upcycled Food Association.

The group began working on third-party certification for foods with upcycled ingredients, enabling them to add a special logo to their packaging. Certified foods must demonstrate environmental benefits. Since then, the association has certified 140 products, including EverGrain from AB InBev's spent grain project and many other products ranging from cans of chopped green-bean offcuts that are not usually included to drinks made from avocado seeds. These products are called upcycled because they enter the human food chain directly, and also help to cut greenhouse gas emissions.

Byproducts from their manufacture are used in a meat-free pot pie made by Birds Eye, and in protein powders made by Nestlé's Garden of Life brand. However, upcycling is crippled by many technical challenges. For example, barley becomes vulnerable to spoilage once it has been steeped in wort to make beer and so requires further preventive processing. Studies show that barley can be a potentially significant contributor to the fast-growing plant protein industry.

If the world's breweries all upcycled their barley, the size of the current plant protein sector would double. There is also potential to upcycle food byproducts into other industries. Food wastes have been upcycled to bioactive compounds for pharmaceuticals while plant fibers have been made into dishware, plastics, or clothing. However, further progress is dependent on advancements in technology.

Often, there are eyebrows raised over the commercial viability of these upcycled food products. Marmite is a rare example of a popular brand that is open about its status as a byproduct. This brewer's yeast is an upcycled foodstuff that has achieved long-term commercial viability for its manufacturer, Unilever. It has been on sale for 118 years. The main challenge lies in the cost of processing, preservation, and transport. Still, this idea of upcycling food waste is real and not some outlying environmental movement for the show-off. Change has been given a luxurious room in the automobile industry too. The US carmaker, Ford had experimented in the past with using recycled plastics and recently has refashioned the netting into wire holders.

It weighs just five grams for the sport utility vehicle. Retrieving waste from the sea and recycling the waste to create new structural components are major steps in reducing carbon footprint. A study conducted by McKinsey estimates that, by 2040, 60 percent of auto industry emissions will come from the materials used in production, unless the automobile industry improvises on sustainability in manufacturing. As per the Circular Car initiative of the World Economic Forum, presently half the cost of a vehicle is spent on materials that will not be recycled.

While carmakers continue to seek ways to cut emissions during driving, there needs to be a simultaneous push to cut them in the supply chain. The plan is to increase the use of materials that can be recycled at the end of a car's life. As we know, the fossil fuel car is the perfect example of linear economy and as we all join hands in combatting the climate crisis, our ultimate goal is to emphasize the circular car. A car that uses materials retrieved from older models in its components or bodywork in an attempt to change the linear 'take-make-dispose' production model is the necessity now.

We must succeed to make a closed-loop system in which materials are reused for the same purpose. Using recycled material opens a door to lower emissions in the supply chain. It reduces the waste load from products that reach the end of their useful life. Recycling although remains a daunting task. Modern cars typically incorporate between 8,000 and 10,000 different materials within them, and the quality needed for automotive parts and car body materials has ruled out the use of recycled materials. However, newer recycling technologies that filter out automotive aluminum from other metals allow carmakers to consider making large parts of their vehicles out of second-hand material.

BMW's i-Vision Circular is made entirely from recycled material. Several carmakers have now produced vision cars to show the potential of recycled materials. Bentley's EXP 100 GT coupé, unveiled at the VW-owned brand's centenary celebration in 2019, contained reclaimed wood around its seats and was coated in paint made from recycled rice husks.

As the actual mystery in making a circular car lies in its battery, several carmaker brands have already taken batteries from used vehicles to make static power storage.

How To Make Money Through Sustainability?

The answer is simple—You just have to use your common sense. We cannot deny that the world revolves around Vitamin M. We all move on the same path of making a profit. While sustainability stages more of a money-saving role on the individualistic front, it has a bigger role at the organizational level.

"Corporate social responsibility isn't just a buzzword anymore. Big or small, retailer or supplier, every company needs to be accountable for its actions. Sound expensive and difficult? Then you're being short-sighted."
– Per Grankvist

Do you know that some of the world's most innovative companies make sustainability a central part of their strategy? And it is not because they are paragons of virtue; rather they are just being sensible in their approach. Sustainability is a common-sense issue instead of a matter of policy and legislation. If we can make it easier to see what needs to be done and how to do it, the much-needed change can be initiated sooner than expected. Sustainability is about conserving resources like how we used to do 100 years ago. Sustainable development is about being able to make free choices now without snatching the same opportunity from our next generation. Conserving resources is everyone's business and we are all capable of doing that irrespective of nationality or culture. Every time we use nature's resources wisely, we save money. And is saving money different from making money? Yes and No. A penny saved today can be used tomorrow for a better cause.

Let me give this common example of resource wastage. It is great to have lights in the bathroom, but is it not wasteful to leave them on when you are not there?

Technology has evolved so much that lights can be controlled by motion sensors. This would conserve your resources and would save money. Making money on sustainability seems like an abstract painting, hard to grasp and fit into our brain. But making money from resources, physical and human, is easy. Every corporation, global or local, is an undemocratic organization that is ruled by money. However, consumers can make them listen through their buying power. Customers have to vote with their wallets and only then will change fall in place.

Sustainability has become a competitive advantage, an opportunity to meet the market's demand in the long term. One company that embraced sustainability as an important part of its brand is the Swedish fashion giant H&M. With its sustainable Conscious Collection, H&M established itself as one of the most progressive fashion companies in the market. Film stars, royalty, and ordinary people are all clamoring to wear the Conscious Collection.

But if you are not a big apparel corporate, then how can you make money? Contemplate your present lifestyle: Do you find any scope?

- Sell your unused clothes

More than 3, 50,000 tons of apparel end up in landfills in a year. If you are looking to clear up space in your wardrobe, do not toss out your unused clothing just yet. Instead of adding weight to the textile waste, you can make a profit off your previously owned clothing by selling them at a consignment shop in your locality.

- Upcycling Business

Transform your waste into something more usable and valuable. Upcycling is a great step you can take toward making fashion more circular and less wasteful. In fact, Etsy and Amazon run a special section for selling upcycled products.

- Do You Have a Green Thumb?

Grow your garden and work over organic farming. You can sell your produce in the local farmer's market.

You can also try cultivating indoor and outdoor ornamental plants and selling them as cut plants or seedlings.

- Start a business of DIY Home décor

Home decors from recycled products are becoming a fad these days. The possibilities are endless as long as you are creative! Once you have finished making recycled handmade crafts, you can try selling them on sites like Etsy, Folksy, or Amazon Handmade.

- Set your sustainable living startup

Leading a zero-waste lifestyle is currently on the rise as an increasing number of consumers are becoming more aware of environmental problems. One in three persons is leaning toward buying eco-friendly options. Undoubtedly, this presents an opportunity to supply the ever-increasing demand for sustainable alternatives to everyday products. So, if entrepreneurship is your cup of tea, now is the best time to get started on your sustainable living startup. It could be as simple as selling shampoo and conditioner bars, wooden containers, bamboo toothbrushes, steel straws, reusable metal canteens, and other plastic-free alternatives. You could also sell eco-friendly tote bags upcycled from old clothes or reusable period pads. While selling zero-waste products to your customers, you may also offer tips and advice on how to live sustainably.

- Invest in Green Enterprises

If the stock market allures you, invest in companies that work on sustainability programs. The past few years have seen an increase in eco-investing opportunities, with eco-minded consumers and investors throwing their financial support behind sustainable startups and enterprises. Allot time for researching companies that are devoted to clean energy or eco-friendly business practices. Look up enterprises with green bonds to help you gain some returns while supporting environmental causes.

Let me tell you the story of Binish Desai who has proved the money-making capacity of recycling. At the brink of the Covid pandemic, as factory production fell and most people stayed at home, there was one potential silver lining: nature would benefit. But Binish Desai, head of a recycling business in Valsad, India, was struck by the increased use of plastic during the pandemic. Desai saw a potential use for the plastic face masks he disposed of daily after personal use.

He disinfected and shredded them, then mixed them with byproducts from chewing gum manufacturing and paper mill waste, which act as a binder and pulp. The result was a brick for use in building construction, which turned out to be three times stronger than conventional versions in India. These bricks, which use about 150 to 200 masks per cubic foot and have been used to build houses, schools, and toilets, are now a core part of Desai's business.

He produces 7,000 to 8,000 bricks per day. Nevertheless, innovations like this are tiny compared with the number of single-use plastics made, used, and immediately discarded, because of the pandemic or otherwise. And this trend is counter to the aim of the circular economy to shift production and consumption away from linear take-make-dispose models. Another UK company, ReWorked, holds PPE in quarantine for 72 hours before shredding and molding the waste into plastic boards for use in construction, joinery, and shop fitting.

If you are wondering that sustainability is only providing profit for a company, then you are mistaken. There are several direct and indirect ways by which a sustainable lifestyle can add value to your pocket. For example, reduced obsolescence with built-to-last or reusable products will improve budgets and quality of life. How? As consumers, when we overcome premature obsolescence, we significantly bring down the total ownership costs and deliver higher convenience by avoiding hassles of repairs and returns. On a daily basis, consumers experience a bundle of benefits by keeping a check on their individual preferences and circumstances.

The repair and replacement chores of sustainability expand the options for customized products for home and work. Furthermore, well-made goods and two-in-one products with multiple functions shall bring both aesthetic and utilitarian benefits. Transition to sustainability will bring disruptions by more productive use of resources and thus bring in a stabilizing effect on the economy. Sustainability imparts a breathing room as it deals with the strains of expanding and aging societies.

Right Now, We Need A Cultural Shift

In the current scenario, sustainable living is often linked with one's virtuous skills. If your friend buys a recycled product and shows it to you, it creates a momentary joy on witnessing the creativity. However, it does not instigate you to join the game of sustainable living.

While many boast about their sustainability endeavors, reusing and recycling are not novelties. It has been ingrained in our mindset and genes. Conspicuous consumption has always been a NO-NO in the previous generations. If we look at the past, where repurposing was common, we might make reuse unremarkable and a regular affair again. All we need to do is to change our attitude toward discarded objects. Our material culture must again go back to our sustainable past.

Modern life is object-centered. Citizens of the past used to make their own things and they needed to source materials and developed the habit of rationalizing. All I can assure you is our forefathers would be shocked by the modern patchwork-makers who buy new fabrics to chop into scraps.

Thinking about the potential of materials, rather than the finished objects, is what we need right now. It provides room to develop new skills, helps protect the environment, and promotes the continual circulation we see in nature. It is a habit we would all do well to reacquire.

We must encourage an economy that aims to 'design out' the waste. A closed-loop circular economy gathers momentum as the products are designed and optimized for a cycle of disassembly and reuse. On the same note, circularity introduces a strict differentiation between consumable and durable components of a product. Once we make the consumables with biological ingredients, we stand on the same line as that of a sustainable lifestyle.

The products are non-toxic and possibly even beneficial, and can be safely returned to the biosphere directly or in a shaft of consecutive uses. The use of recyclable components and renewable sources of energy in the production cycle needs to be incorporated into the production culture. However, every consumable is bound to have some non-degradable element into it. Sustainability and circularity replace the concept of a consumer with that of a user. Will you accept this proposal? This calls for a new contract between businesses and their customers based on product performance. In contrast to the 'buy-and-consume' economy, durable products are leased, rented, or shared wherever possible.

Sustainability is a pill that human society must swallow now. We have to understand that we are not yet lost completely. We have to redirect our thought process and inculcate sustainability as the new normal. It is true that not every individual can become a Binish Desai and provide a solution to the waste management problem.

However, we can at least find out different resources to understand where we are lacking. We can at least get in touch with different organizations that run the business of repair and recycling. It is the mindset that matters now. Either we change our outlook or nature is all prepared to allow the whole of humanity to rot. Today, as you go through various options for a new washing machine, just have a look at your existing one. Are you going to throw that away, just because a new model has come into the market?

If yes, then understand that every material around you has a Plan B; however, there is no Planet B.

7

The Clarion Call

The world has unanimously blamed the caves of Yunnan province for breeding this dreadful life-snatching coronavirus. But is it a creation of nature? The virus is of course a product of our ecosystem; however, the crisis is not. We, humans, have encroached into the natural world and have caused severe environmental damage. Do you know the larger truth behind the huge economic cost of the coronavirus pandemic? *We pay dearly as and when we destroy nature!*

If you still think that this sudden emergence of COVID-19 is a mere act of nature, then let me tell you, such atrocious affairs have always been looming around the corner. We have always turned a blind eye toward them. We let the Antarctic ice melt and watched those breathtaking documentaries on National Geographic Channel only to pass time. We look at our littered streets and complain about municipalities not doing enough, and then, empty our wastes into the already overflowing dustbin on the corner of the road. Have you read the book Spillover by David Quammen? It elaborates on the dramatic rise in human infections and relates it to the alterations humans have caused in the ecosystem.

159

*"We disrupt ecosystems, and we shake viruses loose from their natural
hosts. When that happens, they need a new host. Often, we are it."*
— David Quammen

Call it ALARMING and the term will sound paltry amid the dark
dungeon of the crisis. Humans are now thrown into an
unfathomable den of adversities. The situation is worsening with
each passing day only to prove our crippled resilience. If you think,
you can spend the rest of your life just acknowledging the impending
doom, you are just proving yourself to be a bonehead and nothing
else. We have incensed nature and now she is inflicting this
unbearable pain upon all living beings on Earth. Just think once
about those innocent animals who are killed in the drought and
wildfires. Did they cause global warming? No.

Humans have been the indirect instigators of all their pain. The
present outrageous scenario is an outcome of our unsustainable
growth, and on a similar note, we cannot undo the growth as there
is no concept of anti-growth in the scope of our survival.

Since 1970, a curious question has often floated around. Does
nature try to put a constraint on human growth? This miasma of
natural calamities is more like nature's vocabulary to warn us about
our uncontrolled growth. We cannot undo what has been done.
However, we have to chalk out a balance where human growth can
happen at a reasonable pace while looking after the natural balance.

The emergence of new diseases is just the beginning. From
coastal erosion to the decline of natural resources—fisheries and
forests—the loss of nature carries a huge socio-economic cost. The
World Wildlife Fund (WWF), an international non-governmental
conservation organization, has projected that the total cost over the
next 30 years could be as much as 8 trillion pounds. There are many
intellectuals who disagree with the moral imperative to preserve the
natural world and the global commons; however, there can be no
disagreement on the economic stipulation for doing so. There is an
utter urgency to act with speed and at scale. Our economy is a
wholly-owned subsidiary of nature and not the other way round.

No matter how much humanity advances through technology, we shall always remain at nature's mercy. And right now, we are on the verge of bankruptcy. So, what can we do when the alarms are blaring on our threshold? The party is over now. Humans have been arrogant and disrespectful toward nature. Over the decades, Mother Earth has been patient with us and has given us more than enough chances to rectify our ill-doings.

Did we do anything? The answer is loud and clear; whatever we did has not been enough. We are in dire need of resetting our relationship with nature by valuing it for the indispensable resource that it is. Rather than destroying our natural world, it is now imperative to apply nature-based solutions to our greatest challenges. We must churn our creativity to put in place robust resilience to systemic shocks in the future. Whether you are thinking at your personal level or wish to make a change on the global stage, your small steps contribute toward a larger goal. Sustainability, though, seems a new concept from the environmental protection perspective as far as Anglo-Saxon languages are concerned; however, it came into the vocabulary around the 1710s, even before the invention of the steam engine. Do not nurture that utopian idea of everything shall be fine soon. Nothing will be fine until we make sustainability work.

We must join hands in the restoration of forests, wetlands, and peatlands in our countryside to help regulate water supply and protect communities from floods and landslides. Protecting and restoring coastal ecosystems, such as reefs and salt marshes, which guard the coasts against storm surges and erosion are the need of the hour. Merely watching the consequences of natural calamities on the other side of the world is not going to do us any good. If today, Brazil is swimming through floods, very soon, it will knock at your door too. In our pursuit of making human life better on Earth, we have encroached on innumerable natural habitats. It would take several centuries to read out the list of atrocities humans have committed against nature; however, now is the time to take collective action to turn back the tide.

"The world is reaching the tipping point beyond which climate change may become irreversible. If this happens, we risk denying present and future generations the right to a healthy and sustainable planet – the whole of humanity stands to lose."

– Kofi Annan

If we wish to resolve the climate crisis, we have to carry a polygonal approach. With consumerism waving at us from the pinnacle, we must thrive to reduce inequality and maintain the wealth of the nations to feed a growing global population. We must protect, restore, and sustainably manage nature. The climate crisis has become so obtrusive that no one can claim to be less bad than the others. Both at the personal and organizational levels, each individual has to do everything that is possibly good for natural restoration.

We need to actively reverse the damage we have caused. Besides being the right thing to do, this also makes sense from the economic aspect. The cost of our inaction is becoming too high. The World Economic Forum's Nature Risk Rising report has identified more than half of global GDP as moderately or highly dependent on nature.

The greatest investment of humans will be to embrace nature as a solution. Believe me, investing in nature is going to pay handsome dividends. We have allowed this climate crisis to unfold and now it has crossed the ultimate level, so much so that the human race stands in danger of extinction.

So, what measures have we been taking? According to the reports by The Food and Land Use Coalition (FOLU), a $350 billion annual investment in climate solutions would unlock $4.5 trillion in new business opportunities and would save $5.7 trillion of damage to people and the planet by 2030. The World Economic Forum has even estimated that the nature-positive economy could create nearly 400 million jobs in the next 10 years. The summer fires in Brazil and Siberia, sudden floods in Uttarakhand, India, the rising number of wildfires, and the cruel winters and shrinking monsoons invariably remind us that we are running out of time .

To combat this global problem, we all have to step up to act with courage and urgency. And without keeping nature and nature-based solutions at the forefront and in the center of decision-making, no country, no government can ever meet the 1.5C climate targets set in the Paris Climate Agreement of 2015. We are on the verge of a catastrophic loss of biodiversity, which has now been named the sixth great extinction on Earth.

Do you know about the utopian idea to counter the sixth extinction? Some people are quite vocal about the idea of setting aside half of the earth for nature to breathe and rejuvenate itself and utilize only the remaining half. Is this possible to implement? In this case scenario, only one side of Earth will have ecological balance while the other side, where the humans will be placed, will have nothing but machines and technology. The idea is as impossible as taking your face near a car exhaust and trying to breathe.

Besides running the vicious cycle of demand and supply and sucking on the ultra-consumeristic nature of commoners, businesses have an indispensable role to play. First, they should get their own houses in order, individually and collectively, by acting together across their value chains and with each other to become nature-positive and carbon-neutral. They have to give back to nature and the climate more than they take from it. The fashion and food industries have already set some excellent examples of sustainable and climate-friendly business models. And we need some more.

"It's not that the world hasn't had more carbon dioxide, it's not that the world hasn't been warmer. The problem is the speed at which things are changing. We are inducing a sixth mass extinction event kind of by accident and we don't want to be the 'extinctee.'"

– Bill Nye

Nature Is Everyone's Business

The last 50 years have witnessed an extraordinary change in the way humans have treated nature and how nature has retorted back.

The global economy has expanded four-fold, and over a billion people have been lifted out of extreme poverty. We indeed live significantly longer and childbirth mortality had significantly dropped. However, this 19th and 20th century model of economic growth has come at a significant cost to nature. Here, I can draw an analogy from Mahabharata. To quench the thirst for power between brothers, Kurukshetra witnessed thousands and thousands of lives burning on the funeral pyres. Similarly, in our pursuit to make economic advancements, we have damaged thousands of natural habitats and have created an irrevocable imbalance.

Global statistics prove that nature is declining at rates unprecedented in human history, with up to 1 million species at risk of extinction due to human activity. Unprecedented forest fires from the Arctic to the Amazon, Africa, and Australia have killed billions of animals, destroyed lives, and wiped out huge areas of forest. Do you know that, since 1970, there has been a 60 percent decline in the average population across all vertebrate species? Moreover, during the same period, we have lost more than half of the world's coral reefs and over a third of all wetlands. Meanwhile, greenhouse gas emissions continue to rise and this, in turn, has intensified extreme weather events and nature loss. In short, the whole proclamation of the Paris Agreement is going for a toss.

The World Economic Forum's Global Risks Report 2020 ranked biodiversity loss as one of the top five risks in the coming decade. In our planetary history, humans are now tagged as the drivers of climate and environmental change. The scientific community has named our times as the Anthropocene era. Earth system scientists and researchers have highlighted that if the current rate of nature destruction continues, some biomes like the tundra, grasslands, coral reefs, forests, and deserts will cross irreversible tipping points.

Nearly 17 percent of forest cover in the Amazon has been destroyed since 1970, leave alone in the other parts of the world. We have to acknowledge that the challenges of nature loss are wicked, life-threatening, and convoluted. Not a single business or a human being can detach their dependency from nature.

If we analyze the impact of natural calamities on the global economic status, then we can see that $44 trillion of economic value generation and over half the world's total GDP is moderately or highly dependent on nature and its services, and therefore exposed to risks from nature loss. Intensive mono-cropping, industrial-scale fisheries, and unsustainable construction have further exposed economies and societal well-being to nature-related risks.

"We economists see nature, when we see it at all, as a backdrop from which resources and services can be drawn in isolation."
– Partha Dasgupta

Right now, we are running against time to reset humanity's relationship with nature. Over the coming year, we must come forward with some strict decisions that will define the direction of our planet's future. We do have a chance to bring the environmental and sustainable development agendas together and deliver an ambitious and science-based deal to heal our Mother Earth. Under the UN Climate Convention, a global biodiversity framework has been made to fulfill the Paris Agreement target and embrace nature-based solutions. Amid the miasma of dramatic climate changes, each government is trying to do its bit while a big chunk of the solution lies in the hands of business organizations and our consumeristic mindset.

With each passing year, we can identify a gradual shift in the way countries and companies look at climate change. Numerous companies are working toward halting and reversing nature loss and securing a zero-net-emissions world by 2050. The present time provides a unique opportunity to set in motion systemic changes for the coming decade for moving toward a nature-positive economy. We must identify new mechanisms for financing and collaboration that are public-private and inspire a shared narrative for halting, restoring, and reversing the current rate of nature loss and climate change.

We accept that businesses create value to support a well-functioning society, which in turn flourishes within a delicate balance with the rest of the living beings on the planet. It is imperative that our business and economic structures reflect the necessity of maintaining this balance. Let us look at the example of Nestlé restoring more than 2,400 hectares of native forest along the Kinabatangan River in Malaysia by incentivizing local people to plant trees. In Mongolia, the luxury fashion brand Kering reduced grazing pressure on native grasslands and lowered costs by teaching innovative herding and packing methods to cashmere farmers. Such initiatives are the need of the hour. We need to expand and accelerate our efforts dramatically. There prevails a dearth of effective governance around the world today and we certainly need, now more than ever, courageous business leaders to speak up and advocate for the right actions and policies. They must use their voices and commitment to hasten and bring about the much-needed ambitious political actions.

We have indubitably understood the magnitude of nature's wrath if we make it our enemy. If we instead make nature our ally and lend a hand to create healthy societies, resilient economies, and thriving businesses, there is still hope to avoid extinction. And once we overcome this terrible phase, the world around us will be more inclusive, healthier, equitable, and prosperous.

Have We Destroyed The Environment Unknowingly?

"Man is a very strange creature! He wants to be on a floating ship in the sea while sitting on the shore; and while sitting on the ship, he wants to be sitting on a fixed bench on the shore!"
— Mehmet Murat ildan

There is absolutely no end to human desires. Today, you may want to live on the 25th floor of a condominium and look at the glittering city lights and tomorrow you will be bored while cocooned inside an AC room and would like to go far into the countryside.

Humans are fickle and this constant need to try something new has been a blessing as well as a curse. Do you know that half of the things that have contributed to climate change are an outcome of our ignorance? Let us talk about the construction of huge residential complexes. With the rise in our income levels, we have unknowingly nurtured our dreams to transform small towns into big cities. We have created desired living conditions by building grand houses and cities, and have thereby increased the demand for wood. What is the net outcome of this desire? We have threatened our forests. Logging activities are on the rise, and there is little emphasis on making these forests regain their initial state.

A forest took millions of years to prosper; will you be alive to see the sapling you planted today grow into a forest? No. Should we not curtail this by making sure governments of countries that depend on logging for revenue generation are made to follow due process? We have to embark on afforestation to maintain the carbon cycle and also prevent wind disasters, which these forests aid in.

Now, whom to blame for the plastic? Are we using plastic intentionally? Almost everything comes in plastic packaging now. Items on sale in shops are mostly packaged in plastic containers. Whether you buy a 500 gm packet of peanuts or a packet of wheat flour, everything is wrapped in a plastic cover. Statistically, food packaging accounts for nearly 70 percent of all household trash and waste that eventually end up in landfills.

It is true that plastics are a significant pollutant to the environment due to their inability to degrade quickly and naturally, but are we reducing the amount of plastic production? No. Why? Because plastic has been a boon and we can never deny that. The only possible way is to segregate the plastic waste and subject it to recycling. If we do not do this and are still trying to find an escape route, we are committing the gravest of sins. Our improper disposal of batteries and printer ink cartridges has its own repercussions. Household batteries contain traces of mercury and other toxic chemicals, which damage wildlife and sea life when they accumulate and leak into ecosystems due to faulty and careless disposal.

Ink cartridges, on the other hand, have a more toxic effect on the environment when not disposed of correctly. Similarly, the environmental impact of paint is bewildering. Do you remember Shah Rukh Khan featuring in an advert for a paint company that had introduced the anti-fume variety? Traditional painting materials can have severe harmful effects on the environment, including those from the use of lead and other harmful additives. Lead causes an adverse impact on the environment, and measures need to be taken to reduce its environmental impact. We are inherently stingy in our attitude. We would spend lakhs for a gold necklace but will hesitate to use environment-friendly paint because it is expensive.

Pesticides can cause contamination of land and water when they escape from the production sites and storage tanks and run off into fields. Some pesticides are the cause of global warming and the depletion of the ozone layer. Ozone layer depletion is causing the main harm and danger to our atmosphere and environment, and thus, our environment is being destroyed. And then what if I say, your face wash is a pollutant? Will you throw it out of your bathroom shelf?

People use face washes that mostly contain plastic microbeads, which have been causing a severe environmental problem. The beads are not filtered during sewage treatment due to their small size. When they get released into water bodies, they are swallowed by fish and other marine animals, and this damages their gills. These harmful beads also destroy the animal's internal systems as they are made for the purpose of scrubbing. So, the beads in your face wash, which are meant to clear your pores and make you look fresh, are actually scrubbing and damaging the aquatic animals.

At this juncture, we all understand that the answer to fossil fuel emissions is renewable energy. However, do we realize that acknowledging the present need is far from the reality of implementation? The human world has bigger power plays than a mere cricket match. Though every human, irrespective of nationality and religion, has the same basic need, the duties seem to be different and sometimes unachievable.

The developing nations are always at a disadvantageous position. Let us bring the statistics onto the front page. The amount of arable and non-arable land available per person shows a lopsided scenario. The developed nations who remain the first and the worst polluters get a fair share to combat the climate crisis as their population is less when compared to their available land area. Nobody can deny the role of the growing population in developing nations.

The need for food security is so hefty that no one can dare think of using a mass of land for generating electricity. You all would have seen those videos of Denmark's Wind Energy harvest. It certainly looks amazing, yet not implementable in a country like India whose population is almost 230 times that of Denmark's. Moreover, the availability of the non-arable lands is too meager, and this too is often converted to arable land with better utilization of the water resources.

Now, does this sound like complaining against the developed nations? No. It is about giving a factual analysis of where we have been lacking. A gas based power station needs about 100 acres per 1000 MW; however, the scenario is different for starting a solar power generation station, which needs 4 acres of land for every 1 MW power generation. The same kind of demand prevails in wind energy harvesting too. Now, the existing scenario is that the power consumption of Indians is about one-fourth of what an American or a European would consume and just about half of that of a Chinese. This shows that this country needs tremendous amounts of further energy production to uplift the GDP at least to a respectable level and to give a decent level of human development.

Thus, with such huge needs for power and food and with the lowest availability of land we can neither become exclusive toward renewable energy nor are we willing to become. In any case, our dependence on fossil fuel resources is irrefutable and we cannot clip it down any time soon. The only ray of hope remains in our nuclear power capabilities. However, a tremendous amount of international politics is involved in nuclear power generation in the case of developing countries.

Can we forget the amount of paid resistance that occurred in the case of the Koodankulam Power Station? India is in a catch 22 situation. And in my opinion, it is atrocious for developed nations to ask fledgling nations like India with innumerable constraints to refrain from fossil fuel consumption and reduce the pollution levels. Moreover, the availability of technology plays a crucial role in all those powerful nations. They have advanced technologies to combat pollution issues emanating out of fossil fuel burning. The technology disparity is so awfully visible that Barack Obama had acknowledged the problem and agreed to give the financial cushion toward technology transfer to many nations like India. In the recent Glasgow meet, the sheer need for technology transfer was understood and during the COP27 in EGYPT, the financial assistance has been approved.

The problem at our doorstep is enormous. Climate Change cannot be combatted or confronted single-handedly. Governments, Institutions and public at large must come together with the same vigor. Climate change needs a multipronged coordination and well strategized response from all the key stakeholders; be it governmental bodies or an individual. On the other hand, Governments' responsibility is more crucial in this scenario. While circular economy is one way of tackling the issue, there are some other vital steps as follows that governing bodies can look into.

1. The star rating of power gadgets has to be implemented with utmost alacrity. Further any gadget with 3 star or below must be discouraged or even banned for whatever advantage they may come up with initial costing.

2. Every city administration must implement the concept of segregation and collection system of the solid refuse from the households. The private players must be encouraged to take hold of these refuse and come up with reuse or remake alternatives. It may probably need some grants and assistance in the implementation.

3. The governing bodies and common citizens must understand that there is no alternative to an efficient Public Transportation System. The savings on fuel front and thereby reduction in carbon foot print is enormous. No sane mind will opt for using his own mode of transportation if a good public transportation is available for daily chores. Many European countries are running on public transport. In fact, Mumbai cannot be imagined without shuttle trains.

4. Power production must be judiciously migrated from fossil fuel to renewable sources and nuclear alternatives. India has done some commendable work on this front but still much more is needed to be done.

5. Huge commercial buildings are having 100 percent glass cladding in their design and it has become a norm in the developing country like India. This is not a question of affordability, rather it hovers around the availability of valuable resources like power needed for both illumination and cooling. Tropical country like India is totally unsuitable for such designs. These buildings become enormous power guzzlers. They must be restricted to say 50 percent of the surface area by the City Municipal Authorities.

6. Deforestation (for any purpose) must be totally discouraged. Many state governments justify their role by promoting afforestation; however, we must understand that planting trees is not same as growing a forest. The difference is more than 200 years. Hence, afforestation straightway does not lead to creation of forests. It needs hundreds of years to form its own ecosystem. Moreover, there must be sustainable forest products development movement so that the tribal people do not run into loss as deforestation is prohibited.

7. Water is one of the most mishandled resources. Many studies have univocally concluded that city authorities waste more 30 to 40 percent of the treated water while conveying via pipelines.

8. There must be a premium placed on such scarce resource and hence the authorities must be encouraged to cut the wastages. Piped water must be made available at every nook and corner of the city or town so that it improves the health condition of the citizens and obviates the usage of unhealthy bottled water.

9. Encouraging organic farming has its fair share of pros and cons. It is glaring to see the situation prevailing in Sri Lanka. The country opted for an overnight switch to organic farming without digging much into its unintended consequences. And in 2022, the entire country has now come to a grinding halt due to collapsed economy.

Any change can be implemented only gradually. The present scenario demands that every human should pursue a world where the environment will not need protection. Every country, every individual must come forward with only one policy—preserve Mother Earth. No country, developing or developed, can sustain long enough if we do not join hands to combat the climate crisis. *The idea is we have to walk first to start running.*

Are Humans Becoming Thanos?

Our immediate ecosystem in which we reside forms the fabric of our life. In the last few decades, human actions have shaken up (for the worse) different ecosystems around the globe. Since the 1970s, human pressure on the environment has increased by leaps and bounds without our realizing the pitfalls of the same.

A classic example is the induced smog of Los Angeles in the 70s, which was primarily caused by the intense lobbying of the automobile companies and the oil giants in USA to sell more cars and oil. What the administrators failed to realize was not only did it severely stunt the growth of the public transport system, it also placed undue pressure on the ecosystem. Many trees were chopped to make way for sprawling roads, car parks, and exit ramps.

To cash in, automobile makers started churning out substandard products. People were left with no choice but to keep on buying cars and oil and as a result, there was a severe smog situation. Recent reports estimate that close to 250,000 people directly or indirectly lost their lives from being exposed to these hazardous smog particles. The lesson to be learned from this fiasco is that once we lose large portions of the natural world, there will consequently be a severe reduction in the quality of our life, not to mention the threat to the lives of future generations. Considering the extent of damage caused, it is more like humans are playing the game of Russian roulette.

Earth's population has been growing and so the consumption rate has increased too. The world is increasingly managed in a way that maximizes the flow of material from nature to meet the rising human demand for resources like food, energy, and timber. And in this process, humans have directly altered at least 70 percent of Earth's land, which was mainly for growing plants and keeping animals. Human activities led to deforestation, degradation of land, loss of biodiversity, and pollution, and these have created the biggest impacts on land and freshwater ecosystems. Over the last 50 years, nature's capacity to support us has plunged. Air and water quality is declining, the soil is being depleted, crops are short of pollinators, and coasts are less protected from storms. Can you believe that about 77 percent of rivers longer than 1,000 km no longer flow freely from source to sea? Overfishing has led to ocean change and 66 percent of the ocean's surface has also been affected by other processes like runoff from agriculture and plastic pollution.

Live coral cover on reefs has nearly halved in the past 150 years and is predicted to disappear completely within the next 80 years. Turn the pages of any ecology book and you will realize that coral reefs are home to some of the most diverse ecosystems on the planet. Moreover, the number of alien species has risen. How long did it take for Covid to turn into Omicron? Humans cause the migration of organisms around the world, and this disrupts and often diminishes the richness of the local biodiversity.

And then, human-driven changes in habitats also threaten many endemic species. There lies a myriad of causes: demographic, economic, political, and institutional arrangements underpinned by social values, which interact with one another and bring about such drastic changes on Earth. Sometimes, it feels like humans have taken the role of Thanos, the mad Titan, who thinks it is his responsibility to clear some lives to make life better for the others.

Believe me, the reality is not a Marvel comic. Man has evolved from a primitive being to becoming one with exceptional intelligence. Humans inadvertently discovered fire when rubbing two stones together and the resulting sparks set alight the nearby dry leaves and twigs. Ever since then, humankind's activities have been targeted toward one thing and one thing only—personal upliftment at any cost. We have managed to desecrate the very thing that provides us our daily sustenance by horribly mistreating it in the process.

The discovery of fire led to the creation of refined metal. Metal forges were increased in size to create more refined metal. The ground was dug up to mine for more ore, with not a second thought to the millions of other species that might have inhabited the area. Once metal bent to the will of man, it was only a matter of time before the hubris led to humans believing that mankind was all-powerful and could do anything sans repercussions. Sadly, nothing could be further from the truth.

Humans must realize that they cannot hope to survive without being in sync with the other ecosystems. As stated before, in the process of subjugating and abusing the bounty of nature, humans began trading in these resources. Often dreading to venture too far from the coastlines, the greed to earn more and trade more led to the creation of building larger crafts. Initially, this was achieved by hewing down large trees to build stout vessels. Swathes of forests were cut down, destroying the habitat of birds, bees, and other animals. As time progressed, this took the form of oil-guzzling monstrosities that belch out black smoke while traversing the oceans. Scant regard is paid to marine life.

Several reports exist that talk of whales, manatees, and dolphins that have been injured by the propellers of these leviathan ships. The anti-rust coating on the hulls of these ships is also suspected to kill marine phytoplankton (the largest absorbers of carbon dioxide).

Trading overseas has increased by 900 percent since the beginning of the post-industrial era and the extraction of living materials from nature has risen by 200 percent. The growing physical distance between suppliers and consumers prevents commoners from seeing the destruction caused by their consumption. Before globalization gained significance, humans used to look after the environment around them because their local environment was the only source of their every need. But with globalization, we have massive environmental impacts a long way from where we live. The common man is often insulated from the actual impact as that remains abstract to him.

The pressure for material goods comes mostly from middle- and high-income countries and is often met by low- and middle-income countries. Statistically, Japan, USA, and Europe alone consumed 64 percent of the world's imports of fish products. High-income countries have their own fisheries but most of these have already collapsed. Fishing now takes place in previously unexploited or underexploited fisheries, most of which belong to low-income countries. With the massive increase in trade, sustainability has become a difficult choice to make. Precisely, overexploitation of natural resources happening at another corner of the world leaves a profound impact somewhere else.

On the contrary when we look at the larger picture, the poor nations did benefit economically by becoming the manufacturing units for the rich nations. But in return, they are paying heavy price as the local environment is facing the wrath. In countries like China, many cities have turned into hell-holes due to raid industrialization. With drastic increase in factories and impulsive indulgence into import and export, the economy prospered handsomely. Numerous jobs have been created while imporving the financial status of the country.

However, the impact on the environment has been blissfully forgotten. Currently, humanity is facing three critical scenarios— Global sustainability, Regional competition, and Economic optimism. The whole world must shift toward sustainability by respecting environmental boundaries while making sure economic development includes everyone. Wealth has to be distributed evenly.

Resources and energy should be used judiciously and we all must emphasize economic growth through circularity. Improper education has been a problem for the lower-income countries, which in turn paves the route for developed nations to thrust their damage on the others. This temperament is going to cause further deterioration in the future generation. Nevertheless, as the world places its faith in new and innovative technologies, it will help us cope with environmental problems. Emissions will continue, but newer technologies shall combat the problem.

Combating the loss of ecosystems is a delicate and complex issue and will require a nexus approach. We have to ponder upon how different components of the problem, such as nature, politics, and socioeconomics, all interact with one another. We have to reduce biodiversity loss by changing how we farm, while making sure people have enough food. The societal perspective must see that people's livelihoods are not undermined and social conflicts are not aggravated.

These issues can be handled if we focus on regenerating and restoring high-carbon ecosystems, such as forests and wetlands. Similarly, the need for food could be met by changing dietary choices and reducing waste. However, in order to achieve this fully, the world needs to reevaluate current political structures and societal norms. In the past 60 years, 60 percent of the Earth's ecosystem has been degraded. Our natural ecosystems are finding it hard to cope with the different pressures and are unable to adjust. If we continue depleting resources and destroying our environment, soon it will be too late for all of us to recover. It is not an exaggeration when I say that we are well on our way to our own destruction, slowly and surely.

And our courage lies in accepting our mistakes and moving forward toward a sustainable solution. Efforts are already being made to address these global concerns. People are becoming more aware that the little things you do every day do have an effect. We have to understand that every aspect of our ecosystem is important as when one gets destroyed, the rest will follow. Imagine if all the carnivores vanish from Earth. Can you not feel the drastic alteration in the food chain? The consequences of human actions and climate change are blaring at our doorstep. It is high time we choose to thrive in a sustainable environment. No contribution is insignificant. In everything you do, think of its impact on you, the society at large, and of course nature.

The Ripple Effect

We humans want money and life and our needs have slowly become unquenchable, to say the least. Moreover, as I see it, the main trouble is we have developed a knack for choosing everything that invariably harms us in some way or the other.

Have you ever thrown a pebble into a pond? Even a minuscule act of yours has a ripple effect on Mother Earth. Whether you buy a packet of Kurkure or get your old microwave oven repaired, you are impacting the environment in either a good or a bad way. Let us talk about the new novel you have purchased. It is about five inches by eight, quite compact, and pleasant to hold.

The words printed in crisp dark ink on the cream-colored paper create a vivid impression, so much so that every character moves before you like in a movie. The graphic designer has done a wonderful piece of artwork and the jacket looks colorful in its sturdy cardboard cover. This is how a book is usually made: an intelligently conceived object while keeping portability and durability in mind. Though attractive and durable, this book will not last forever, maybe not even through your life span. So, what happens when it is discarded?

The paper came from trees, so you have already played a role in depleting natural diversity and soil. Still, paper is biodegradable, but the ink that has been used to print so crisply on the paper and create the striking image on the jacket contains carbon black and heavy metals. The jacket is not really paper, but an amalgam of materials: wood pulp, polymers, and coatings, as well as inks, heavy metals, and halogenated hydrocarbons. It cannot be safely composted, and if it is burned, it produces dioxins, which are potent carcinogens. Thus, you can see how discarding a simple novel can have a ripple effect on so many aspects of life.

The global situation, at present, demands a closed loop of demand and supply and has become quite loud about circular economy: every step of ours matters to the world. Even though sustainability has been considered as the development of products, goods, and services that meet our present needs without compromising the ability of future generations to fulfill their own needs, it produces a ripple effect toward the larger goal. Sustainability recognizes that the environment is an exhaustible resource.

Therefore, it is important to use the environment and its resources rationally and protect it for the good of the Earth, our environment, humanity, and all living things. Irrespective of each scientific development that we target toward combating the various problems of climate change, we have to be ready to innovate further. Every invention will come with its distinct set of pros and cons and this is inevitable.

When the petrol engine was invented, the scientists never left the room for innovation and sought after efficiency and constructed diesel engine. Every invention comes with a lot of room for improvement and our job as humans is to work on that scope for improvement. The principles of sustainability revolve around the science of combating this prevailing crisis. The concept indeed demands that we change, and change is messy, difficult, and needs an extra effort. Nevertheless, sustainability has come up as the only way out of this mess.

Today, while most people associate the science of sustainability with the environment, we have to take a deeper look at its influence over other contexts as well. Sustainability plays a vital role in economic development while fulfilling humans' social responsibility. It reflects upon humans' endeavor to preserve Mother Earth while abandoning the anthropocentric nature.

In a sustainable society, humans live in harmony with the natural environment, conserving resources for their future generations, so that everyone enjoys social justice and high quality of life. Sustainability improves the quality of our lives, protects our ecosystem, and preserves natural resources to ensure a balance amongst all forms of life. Additionally, in the corporate world, sustainability showcases an organization's holistic approach from manufacturing to logistics to customer service. There is indeed a ripple effect to going green and sustainable. It saves the cost of several operations while benefitting the environment.

No matter where we live or who we are, we all carry a moral obligation to each other, our future generations, and other species to sustain the planet. Our present choices and actions have huge long-term impacts on future generations.

Holding the NIMBY approach may keep your house clean, but the surroundings remain dirty and there the ripple effect starts. You litter the roads with your garbage. A cow shuffles through the garbage and unknowingly eats the plastic bag and dies after a couple of weeks on the same road. Now, can you bear the smell of that putrefying body?

Practicing sustainability ensures that we make ethical choices that bring a safe and livable future to everyone. Today if we deplete the resources of the Earth and still keep giving birth to the future generation, what are we leaving for them? What would happen if all the fish die? You as a human may have other options for food, but we have to realize that there is a marine food chain, which is disrupted. There lies a long-term effect of a sustainable lifestyle. A small step today shall make a huge change tomorrow.

Our society would benefit from improved water and air quality, reduced landfills, and increased renewable energy sources as sustainable actions help make a real difference in society. Being committed to sustainability reduces your carbon footprint and the amount of toxins released into the environment, making it safe. When we focus on sustainability, the entire world benefits and gets to live in clean, healthier living conditions.

To date, if the linear economy has led us into the vicious cycle of use and throw, sustainable lifestyle too is going to impart a ripple effect of benefits. Before you frown at the demands the present world is making on you, understand that sustainability is not about making some histrionic changes in life. Some simple choices can make our life more stable and enjoyable. Choosing to live a sustainable lifestyle does not mean you will have to give things up or reduce your quality of life at all! In fact, you will feel more fulfilled and happier knowing you are contributing to a better world. And that is where the benefits lie.

Encouraging the conservation of natural resources deeply penetrates everyone's thought process if you set an example. If you make sustainability important in your personal life and business, you are bringing a deeply important conversation to the forefront of consumerism. Staging sustainability at every stratum of demand and supply chain is going to have a monumental effect on this race against the climate crisis. No corner of the globe is immune from the devastating consequences of climate change. If you pay close attention, you will be as worried as I sound.

Rising temperatures are fueling environmental degradation, natural disasters, weather extremes, food and water insecurity, economic disruption, and conflicts. Sea levels are rising, the Arctic is melting, coral reefs are dying, oceans are acidifying, and forests are burning, which makes it clear that our dealing with nature is going through a rough patch. As the infinite cost of climate change reaches irreversible highs, it is high time for bold collective action. And while we pause and ponder over the ripple effects of benefits that a sustainable lifestyle can introduce; realize the cynosure of our life.

Mother Earth is not our heirloom; we have not inherited it from our ancestors. Rather, we have borrowed it from the generations to come.

> *"You cannot get through a single day without having an impact on the world around you. What you do makes a difference, and you have to decide what kind of difference you want to make."*
> – Jane Goodall

CONCLUSION

The climate change crisis is not propaganda raised by some attention-seeking environmentalists. It is an overwhelming curse for which humans are paying penance. While we glare at our newspapers or stare agape at the television screens on seeing the news of floods and wildfires, we have to understand that the mere acknowledgment of the problem will not fetch us a solution. Humans have this innate desire for seeking a better life for themselves and their kin, that too with no set boundaries. We have embraced the gradual transformation from being the hunted to becoming the hunter and then with unprecedented speed, becoming the producer of microscopic robots with infinite possibilities. And now, the situation demands us to change again.

We have sucked enough from the bosom of Mother Earth for our own selfish needs and in the process have threatened every form of life, including our very own. Amid this evolving crisis on Earth, there is still a ray of hope to overturn the bleak odds and rise above the tide of destruction. Sustainability—the current buzzword and a bright ray of hope amidst all the gloom and murky future. Certain corporations have taken undue advantage of our rising consumeristic pattern and their targeted selling has somehow influenced all of us to go through the take-make-dispose pattern.

Over the years, this linear economy has transformed into a Frankenstein's monster: a hodgepodge of anachronistic ideas and unsustainable methods. The waste generation is slowly moving toward a tipping point. We must redirect our actions toward reducing the amount of waste we generate by thinking differently. Waste must be treated as a resource before we dump it in landfills or send it to incinerators. Production and consumption cycles can no longer run on the treadmill of cradle to grave.

Circular economy is the beginning of a new dawn where one man's waste is another man's treasure, one organization's trash is another organization's feed, and one ecosystem's refuse is another ecosystem's resource. In this concept, the basic tenets of the 3 R's are strictly adhered to. No product is produced unless it is needed (Reduce). No product is disposed of without repairing (Reuse). No disposed product is left untreated (Recycle).

Following these concepts not only brings a reduction in the whopping amount of waste but also adds value to our wallets. A penny saved is always a penny gained. Cradle to Cradle is the new maxim in the production and consumption lifecycle. And lately, the number of R's in a sustainable lifestyle have grown in number. We have to Rethink our consumption rate. We must Refurbish our mindset. We must let biodegradable wastes Rot.

Nature feeds all; from those microscopic bacteria to elephants, nature is the ultimate source of food and living. Somehow, humans have the mistaken notion that they are supreme in this fragile world and their actions have vehemently ruined the entire balance of the natural ecosystem. Our existence is in grave danger and radical solutions must be implemented at both personal and societal levels. No matter who you are, which company you belong to, or how much money you have, everybody has to contribute enough to reduce their carbon footprints. Climate change is akin to the Domino Effect where one simple whim of humans in asking for more, that too ASAP, has led to a series of drastic alterations in every aspect of nature.

Mother Earth is facing three major adversities of climate change, which include nature and biodiversity loss, pollution, and waste. The key instigator of this problem is the unsustainable consumption pattern of humans.

Right now, we are at a crossroads. We can either take the route of sustainability and circularity or we can remain enamored by the route of take and dispose and keep feeding our immoral consumption rate. A sustainable lifestyle is implementable and profit-oriented and anyone with sheer common sense can realize its value amid the prevailing crisis. Sustainable consumption and production must become the new trend in the market to ensure better health for our businesses, people, and the planet. Mother Earth is wailing and urging us to reinvent. Re-Evolution of humans is the need of the hour. It is upon us to decide if we want to change or perish.

"Sustainability is not just about adopting the latest energy-efficient technologies or turning to renewable sources of power. Sustainability is the responsibility of every individual every day. It is about changing our behaviour and mindset to reduce power and water consumption, thereby helping to control emissions and pollution levels"
– Joe Kaeser

REFERENCES

1.

- https://timesofindia.indiatimes.com/city/chennai/climate-change-tamil-nadu-coast-may-witness-heavy-spells-of-rain-in-next-decade/articleshow/88515356.cms
- https://www.ipcc.ch/site/assets/uploads/2018/03/SREX-Chap3_FINAL-1.pdf
- https://www.nrdc.org/stories/flooding-and-climate-change-everything-you-need-know
- https://www.hindustantimes.com/environment/nasa-visualises-how-sea-levels-will-rise-in-indian-coastal-regions-101629257135231.html
- https://www.science.org/doi/full/10.1126/science.aaz9600
- https://www.edf.org/climate/heres-how-climate-change-affects-wildfires
- https://www.bbc.com/news/science-environment-58073295)
- www. ncbi.nlm.nih.gov/pmc/articles/PMC7375877/
- https://www.indiatoday.in/diu/story/how-has-climate-change-affected-indian-cities-1876164-2021
- https://climate.nasa.gov/causes/

2.

- https://css.umich.edu/factsheets/carbon-footprint-factsheet
- https://css.umich.edu/factsheets/carbon-footprint-factsheet
- https://www.sciencedirect.com/topics/social-sciences/anthropocentrism

3.

- https://www.sustainablejungle.com/sustainable-living/what-is-sustainable-living/
- Doughnut Economics: Seven Ways To Think Like A 21st-Century Economist (2017) Kate Raworth, Random House Business Books, pp 42
- https://www.apple.com/environment/pdf/Apple_Environmental_Progress_Report_2021.pdf
- https://www.ikea.com/gb/en/this-is-ikea/about-us/were-all-in-this-together-pubc8331c51
- https://changestarted.com/big-indian-companies-that-have-made-climate-commitments/

4.

- https://ellenmacarthurfoundation.org/topics/circular-economy-introduction/overview
- Towards Circular Economy by Ellen MacArthur Foundation
- Accelerating India's Circular Economy Shift: FICCI Circular Economy Symposium Report

5.

- https://www.nationalgeographic.com/environment/article/plastic-pollution
- https://www.sciencehistory.org/the-history-and-future-of-plastics
- https://www.unep.org/news-and-stories/press-release/global-garbage-crisis-no-time-waste
- https://www.weadapt.org/knowledge-base/cities-and-climate-change/urban-green-infrastructure-an-introduction
- https://www.ft.com/how-to/deal-with-farmers'-love-of-plastic

6.

- https://www.ft.com/carmakers-shift-gear-recycled-product
- https://www.ft.com/upcycling-food-industry
- https://www.ft.com/secondhand-clothing
- https://www.ft.com/right-to-repair
- https://nicholasinstitute.duke.edu/events/impact-climate-change-educational-attainment-evidence-global-tropics

"madhu vātāḥ ṛitāyate madhu kṣaranti sindhavaḥ mādvih naḥ santuṣadhi.

madhu naktamutusāsu madhumatpārthiva rajah madhu kṣorastu suryah mādhirgābo bhavantu naḥ"

Environment provides bliss to people leading their life perfectly. Rivers bliss us with sacred water and provide us health, night, morning, vegetation. Sun bliss us with peaceful life. Our cows provide us milk). The plant ecology has a great importance to keep the environment in balance.

(Rigveda,1/90/6,7,8)

www.ingramcontent.com/pod-product-compliance
Lightning Source LLC
Chambersburg PA
CBHW030010290326
41934CB00005B/287